Cindy's own thoughts combined with those of other Asian TCKs touch our hearts deeply and we trust will also touch the hearts of mission-minded Christians and church mission committees. I hope Growing Up Global will have the widest possible circulation.

James & Leone Taylor, OMF

All these missionary and pastors' kids come from dedicated Christian families. They are taking a great risk in sharing about their lives, even imperfections about themselves and their parents. Yet God's glory is not jeopardized by human imperfections. Like many psalms in the Bible, these genuine stories will leave us with the conviction that God is even more real than ever.

Matthew Mok, Senior Pastor, Shepherd International Church

I am deeply touched by each young writer's courage, perseverance and their positive attitude toward life. As you hold this book in your hand, please bless each of them as you read their stories. They surely are arrows in God's quiver, and trail blazers for the next stage of world missions.

Titus Loong, Director, Wecare Center

As a missionary parent who has raised three TCKs, I appreciate what it means for them to come to terms with who they are. Growing Up Global gives them a voice and helps them to know that they are not alone or strange. In fact, TCKs understand the world from a global perspective and can be key to missions, companies and even governments who have to operate in our interconnected world.

Rich Johnson, WorldVenture

Cindy has not only made it possible for these TCKs to express their reflections on their journeys, she has also let their parents and other Christian readers read between the lines, and be reminded that God has not abandoned those who have so faithfully served Him. God Himself has shepherded these children, led them through thick and thin, and brought them out of confusion into strength and maturity.

Raymond Lo, Executive Director, FEBC HK

Growing Up Global

What a TCK's Life is Like   1st edition 2008, 2nd edition 2009
A Collection of Stories Compiled and Edited by Cindy Loong

Editor   : Cindy Loong
Publisher   : Shepherd International Church Limited
                      Flat 606, Citimark, 28 Yuen Shun Circuit,
                      Sha Tin, New Territories, Hong Kong

Hong Kong Distributor : Hong Kong Association of Christian Missions
                      128 Castle Peak Road, 11/F ,
                      Cheung Sha Wan, Kowloon, Hong Kong
                      Tel: 852-2392 8223   e-mail: info@hkacm.org.hk

Overseas Distributor : Cindyloong@gmail.com

ISBN 978-988-17435-1-0

Growing Up Global

Global

What a TCK's Life is Like

A Collection of Stories Compiled and Edited by Cindy Loong

This book is dedicated to Dr. David Pollock,

who first expressed his passion for TCKs in his book

The Third Culture Kid Experience.

... Contents ...

Making My Faith My Own

Tears to Joy

Spiritual Heritage of TCKs

Foreword

In 1995, Dr. James Taylor, the director of OMF Hong Kong, came with their missionary Polly Chan to my office at the Hong Kong Association of Christian Missions to share their vision about setting up a ministry to care for missionary kids (MKs) in Hong Kong. Thus began my care for TCKs. Over the past thirteen years, many have questioned me, saying, "Mission work is still in its beginning stages, and our resources are so limited. Should we "waste" so much money on this small group of children? Moreover, aren't missionaries supposed to endure hardships? Do their children really need such quality care?" I must admit that these comments came from hearts showing genuine concern for the Great Commission. Yet up until now, I am still strongly convinced of the importance and value of the ministry of TCKs.

This special group of kids, because of their parents' faith and commitment to missions, have struggled to grow up in different cultures. The challenges and confusion they go through are often difficult for others to comprehend. By the grace of our Heavenly Father, the loving care of their parents, support from peers, and support from a group of TCK caregivers, most of these TCKs have been able to overcome bitterness and complaints. They have walked through the shadows, kept their faith, and are accomplishing great things in society, at church, and in God's Kingdom. Many of them are following their parents' footsteps and have become full time Christian workers.

In this book, the TCKs wrote so honestly and openly that I was shocked! What they describe might cause their parents to be somewhat embarrassed. However, let me express my admiration to all the parents mentioned in this book. I fully believe that you have made your best efforts in all these circumstances. Now, when your children can freely and honestly express feelings, it shows they can fully accept and respect you. Therefore, there is no place for guilt, only thanksgiving. Because you first sought His Kingdom and His righteousness, He has given you all that you need.

I finished reading the entire book in a single sitting. Each article, (including my daughter's), struck my heart deeply. I thank Cindy wholeheartedly for compiling this book. Cindy has not only made it possible for these TCKs to express their reflections on their journeys, she has also let their parents and other Christian readers read between the lines, and be reminded that God has not abandoned those who have so faithfully served Him. God Himself has shepherded these children, led them through thick and thin, and brought them out of confusion into strength and maturity.

May God use each story in this book to inspire you to pray more fervently for the growth of TCKs around you, and to care for and support this very special group.

Raymond Lo
Executive Director, FEBC HK

Preface

This book is a collection of stories about the lives of seventeen adult Third Culture Kids (TCKs). A Third Culture Kid is a person who has lived in more than one culture and geographic location during his/her developmental years. TCKs usually have parents who are either involved in the international marketplace, mission work, or pastoral work. They grew up watching their parents lead busy lives of significant influence. What, however, is the purpose of their own lives? In addition, TCKs may spend many years in confusion, not fully understanding the meaning behind their cultural experiences. Many onlookers might also wonder why God has allowed them to go through so many cultural transitions. "Isn't it difficult, too difficult?", they wonder. Yes, it is difficult. However, there is redemption hidden in each TCK story.

The purpose of this book is to encourage TCKs who reads it to discover the meaning of their life, identity, and calling in Christ. God has not only called parents, but He has called them, to know Him, to be known by Him, and make Him known to the world. Throughout the book, many writers communicate their passion to tell the next generation of TCKs, that God's grace is more than sufficient for whatever the TCK life may bring. Here, I would like to thank all contributing writers for being willing to share their stories, and who wrote so honestly and meaningfully.

Doh Ah, Aaron, and Levi share their struggles with adjustment when their family moved around, and how difficult that was. Mabel and Ruth contribute a refreshing honesty of how moving around affected their developmental years. Linda, Elaine and Joshua give us a realistic picture of what it is like to be a TCK in a majority culture. Florence On's (1943-February 2007) life story unfolds God's prophetic purposes in her life, which were fulfilled through a road that for Florence was not always sunny or rosy.

What about the issue of personal faith? Missionary Kids (MKs) and Pastors' Kids (PKs) have watched their parents influence many people spiritually. How have they made their faith their own?   Karen and Jane reflect on the ups and downs of their spiritual journey, leading to a personal experience of God's faithfulness. Titus shares how God intervened in his life in a dramatic way to make sure he knew who was in charge of his life. Julia and Samuel share about the challenges and privileges of being a pastor's son and daughter. My heartfelt thanks to Beth and Moses. They share their stories so honestly and deeply, and yet so beautifully, describing the grace of God that came into their lives, resulting in their personal transformations.

I thank my mom, Helen Loong, for enthusiastically contacting missionaries and pastors to encourage them to get their children to write for this book. I thank my father, Titus Loong, for coaching me in understanding the Asian missionary movement, and for wholeheartedly supporting my ministry, and the publication of this book. Thanks to Dr. James Taylor III for consistently praying for our family and for having a vision for Asian TCK ministry. Thanks also to Raymond Lo and Judy Long for taking the time to write the forwards. Kathy Narramore and Polly Ho have been especially encouraging throughout the whole process of the book's editing, and have reminded me about the importance of this book.

I am grateful to God for the many mentors and friends whom He has given me. My spiritual family in Harvest Rock Church, Pasadena saw me through the first half of my healing process. Although they were not familiar with my kind of TCK upbringing, they cared enough to listen to my experiences. My nurture group in Shepherd International Church saw me through the second half of my healing process, when I sought to pursue a spiritual life in a cross-cultural environment. Thanks to all of you for your prayers, friendship, and support! Elaine Stafford, my TCK friend since childhood, proved to be my primary support when I moved to Hong Kong, as both of us would talk about the trials of being an adult TCK in Asia. Her visits were both therapeutic as well as fun! I could totally be myself around her. My cousin Jennie Ho allowed me to stay at her home in Glendale, California for almost two years, during which I wrote my TCK story and other TCK articles. Her daughter Julie Ho enthusiastically supported the production of this book by contributing her own story as well. Thanks to all of you!

It is my joy to present you with the second edition of Growing Up Global. I would like to thank all those who helped to make these articles into a book. Pak Shem translated some Chinese stories into English. Albert did the layout and publishing. The Johnson family and Daniel Hom helped with the critical final stages of proofreading. Finally, thank you to all who have been praying for and financially supporting TCK ministry. I especially appreciate the HKACM TCK Care Committee for their commitment to TCK care.

Finally, I would like to thank the Lord Jesus for his goodness in my life, enabling me to write my TCK story, and then to compile this volume. As I house sat for my friend in 2005, I asked God about the meaning of my life, and He showed me His perspective. Later, I was inspired by stories from other MKs and PKs that are now compiled into this book. Some of these were my childhood friends! I thank the Lord for their willingness to share their stories so that others ean be comforted and enlightened. Truly, these are testimonies to Jesus' love and faithfulness. I am thankful that the vision He gave me for this book has come to pass. Thank you, Jesus!

Cindy Loong

Hong Kong Association of Christian Missions Member Care Secretary

A Beginning Word

Judy Long

Growing up in Taiwan was a great adventure for our children. They rode bikes, swam at the pool, ate "bings", made friends among the Chinese and aboriginal neighbors, loved Chinese food, played "jen jya" after dinner on the street with other kids, went to the beach, learned to speak Chinese, studied, played music, and then, one day, they left home to go back to the United States. It was a shock for them to start living as adults in their home country. To them, Taiwan was home. They certainly weren't Chinese; but their lives had been shaped in a special way by living in Taiwan.

Sometimes people think that raising children in another country is not fair to the children. "They didn't ask to go; it's your ministry not your children's." Children grow up where their parents live. It's that way for children all over the world. Did God have something else in His plan for them other than living in Taiwan with our family? No. God used the experience of living in another country and culture to make our children very aware of the world outside of the United States. They understand that not everyone lives the same way; that people in different places have different habits and different ways of doing things. They have a world view that includes the whole world.

As a family, we would have a time of Bible reading and prayer each night after dinner. We would pray for friends and family in America, for the people who helped to support us financially, and for our friends in Taiwan. We prayed for people in the hospital who were sick and injured; we prayed for the families of people who had died; we prayed for our Taiwanese friends, that they would understand God's wonderful love for them. These times shaped our children's hearts. They know that God hears prayers and cares about the things that affect our lives.

How did shaping their hearts and minds in this way turn out? They know the Father's heart towards them; repentance and forgiveness when they have strayed are great realities for them. They have courage to follow God's leading, to live in another country and raise their children there; to live simply; to be generous with time, energy, and resources so others can know the love of God. They have confidence in God's love and care for them, so much so that they can take risks in doing God's will without fear. Their faith becomes more robust as they take on the challenges of living for Christ wherever they are. Thank you, God, for making our children people You can use for the work of Your Kingdom! It still amazes me that Beth's story encourages so many parents even today.

I've known Cindy since she was a very little girl. To see her put these stories into print is a great pleasure. She certainly knows the world of MKs from the inside. She is continuing the legacy her parents passed down to her in the world of missions. I know the readers will treasure the insights and wisdom of this collection of stories!

Judy Long and her husband, Bob, a Pediatrician, served with The Evangelical Alliance Mission for 25 years at the Taitung Christian Hospital in Taitung, Taiwan. They also served in Vietnam. Now, they are doing member care for missionaries in Asia. Their home base is Columbia, South Carolina. Two children are currently in Asia, one in Africa, and one in the US.

Moving Again?

The Iceberg

Cindy Loong

According to David Pollock in "The Third Culture Kid Experience",
cultural change and transition affects a person the most during the first 18 years,
because the person is still developing in his/her personality. Kohl's iceberg
illustration explains this phenomenon of "not belonging." (Pollock, p. 40 – 41)

Behavior
Words
Customs
Traditions
Surface culture

Beliefs
Values
Assumptions
Thought processes
Deep culture

L. Robert Kohls suggests we look at culture as a kind of iceberg, with one part clearly visible above the surface of the water, and another, much larger part, hidden below (the line represents water level). The part above the water can be identified as the surface culture, and includes behavior, words, customs, and traditions. Underneath the water, where no one can see, is the deep culture, and it consists of beliefs, values, assumptions, and thought processes. Above is a representation of Kohls' culture iceberg.

In this description, Kohl distinguishes between "surface culture" and "deep culture". Many TCKs have learned to adapt and change their surface culture to blend into the culture around them. However, deep down inside, they know that they do not completely belong. This is because their deep culture will always contain elements of culture from each place where they have lived, from age 0 to 18.

For example, a TCK who is born in Africa and lives there until age twelve, and then relocates to Taiwan with his/her parents, can learn to adjust on the surface. Within one year's time, he/she can be speaking Mandarin and acting like a Taiwanese local person. However, deep down inside, there are still elements of Africa that will always be a part of him/her. Thus, his/her African upbringing becomes a permanent part of his/her identity.

The issue is compounded for TCKs who move multiple times before age eighteen, especially if they attend local instead of international schools. For each place they live in, they pick up a culture that will become a part of their identity. Thus a TCK who grew up in Africa, Hong Kong, and U.S.A., will have a deep sense of belonging to each culture, while at the same time feel that he/she does not fully belong to any of them.

As adults, many TCKs still look for a sense of "settled ness" that will allow their deep culture to be made known to the people around them. After a while, it becomes tiring to always function and relate to people on the surface culture level. Many TCKs feel that people do not completely understand them. This is a normal feeling, considering their deep culture mix.

Many people have labeled TCKs as unstable. In a quest to look for their deep cultural belonging, TCKs may feel a strong urge to revisit every place they have grown up in. However, having visited all these places, their deep cultural problem is still not resolved. They still don't feel like they belong. When they describe this to their non-TCK friends, they are quickly misunderstood and labeled. So, many of them remain silent and do not discuss it. Some TCKs use their learned skills to blend in quickly. Others may move back and forth a few times before they finally settle in one place. The journey of discovery is lonely, often lacking in spiritual and emotional support. Settling in one church, even their parents' home church, can be equally hard at times.

I believe that the quest of TCKs looking for their cultural identity is a deeply spiritual quest. I believe that a person's deep culture encompasses the spiritual life of an individual. The beliefs, values, assumptions, and thought processes of a certain group of people, in fact describe the spiritual DNA of a culture. That is why it is so important to come to terms with one's deep culture. TCKs have a massive challenge ahead of them. This challenge is to process every single "deep culture" element in them and decide which ones they will keep and which ones they will let go. Once they figure out which deep culture elements they will keep, they have only completed half of the process. The next step is to find a way to put these elements together in a completed "puzzle" so that they have a workable deep culture identity. This workable identity is formally known as the "third culture," thus the name Third Culture Kids.

Deep Culture Integration

Deep culture integration is a slow and painful process. Many TCKs have expressed the desire just to blend into the culture around them and not engage in the process. On the surface, this seem to be the best solution, especially if the TCK is not ready to engage in the pain of deep culturae integration. This is understandable. However, sooner or later, the lack of integration will make itself known in the form of a certain "unsettled ness." I am also strongly convinced that there is no way TCKs can come to the fullness of their identity in Christ until they engage in the process of deep culture integration. Until then, the person remains culturally fragmented on the inside. In essence, TCKs who choose not to engage in deep culture integration are trying to be monocultural when in fact they cannot and will never be. For better or for worse, their identity has been permanently affected by more than one culture. It is for better, if they are willing to engage in deep culture integration.

On the other hand, TCKs who are going through the process of deep culture integration will come across as unconventional and even rude at times. The quieter ones will withdraw and refuse to interact socially. Friends and mentors of TCKs must bear in mind that these TCKs are going through a very important season of identity formation, and need as much encouragement and understanding as possible. Moreover, friends and mentors must refrain from treating this process as an emotional problem that must be fixed and gotten over as soon as possible. In fact, the TCK is going through one of the most important stages in their life and spiritual development.

Cultural Icebergs

Just as in the days of the ice age, when icebergs were moving along the surface of the earth and affecting the very boundaries of continents, so we are living in a day and age when the boundaries of cultures are being shifted right before our very eyes. This time, the source of the shift is not physical icebergs but cultural icebergs in the form of TCKs moving from continent to continent!

God deliberately desires for cultures to collide with one another, in order to get rid of racism and ethnic pride in the body of Christ. God has given TCKs the privilege and challenge to stimulate the church. Never before in history has there been a more exciting time as now to be alive as a TCK!

Transition

Doh Ah Kim

It's the people that matter—social, cultural and environmental changes can be dealt with—but without friends, transitions could become unbearable. At each transition in my life, there were a few friends who stuck with me, and were patient even though I did not respond quickly.

My first transition occurred when our family moved to Taiwan. It was perhaps the smoothest one, because I had no idea what was going on. The most difficult transition happened later on during my teenage years. My series of transitions started at the age of four, when our family moved from Korea to Taiwan. Perhaps because I moved at such a young age, I was not aware of the major changes in life I would experience.

I started out at a Chinese kindergarten knowing no Chinese. One day I returned from kindergarten frustrated, locked the door to my room, and started sobbing. Although I cannot remember clearly, even at age four, I knew I did not belong to the group, and most of all, there was nothing more distressing than being forced to take a nap at a place which felt foreign to me. From then on, numerous transitions occurred while moving from one country to another, mostly due to furloughs and changing of schools.

One of the most difficult, yet rewarding transitions was in 1992 during our family's first furlough. During the 18 months in Seoul, we settled in a nice neighborhood apartment complex close to the school I was to attend. I entered 3rd grade elementary school uninformed and naive as to what to expect. I couldn't understand what the teacher was saying when he told us to bring a sketchbook and watercolors to school. I didn't understand why the whole class had to be on detention when the other classmates did not know an answer to a math problem. But during those months, I came to know a classmate named So-young, who lived on the same apartment floor as I. What a comfort it was to see her at my door every morning!

It's the people that matter—social, cultural and environmental changes can be dealt with—but without friends, transitions could become unbearable. At each transition in my life, there were a few friends who stuck with me, and were patient even though I did not respond quickly. During my high school years in Korea (1997-2000), I felt detached from Korean society because I attended an American school (Seoul Foreign School) while living in my home country. This created a gap between myself and other Koreans, especially at church. Yet, there was a girl who would always say "Hi Doh Ah" and smile. I could barely return a smile, because I was miserable. Her persistence for three years saying "Hi Doh Ah" has made us best friends. Now she is in Mongolia, even though we seem to be apart all the time, we keep in touch because of the firm foundation we have established.

My latest transition has been from Calvin College (USA) back to Korea. Now a law school student at Handong International Law School, I can say that my previous transitions back to Korea have been immensely helpful. And God has also faithfully given me great friends, maybe the greatest, since I have met my husband here!

Doh Ah was born in Korea and grew up in Taiwan with her missionary parents. She was educated first in a Chinese school, then at Morrison Christian Academy of Taiwan (American system), Korean high school, Ferndown Upper School (England), Calvin College (MI, USA), and Handong International Law School.   Doh Ah married Soo Seok Yang in July 2007 .

Ugly Duckling

李奕惀 Li Yi Lun

When I was with the children of pastors and missionaries, I recognized my own young shadow in them, just like the story of the ugly duckling who did not know who he was. The duckling put his best effort to intermingle with those who did not know or want to acknowledge him.

Little Ugly Duckling

The Gospel Church of Faith, Hope and Love in Hong Kong was my spiritual home. At the present I am equipping myself in the United States. This is the 10th year. I have had opportunities to serve in different capacities and places. I have experienced the full grace of God and become God's blessing to others. Whenever I come back to my mother church, the Gospel Church of Faith, Hope and Love, I feel like I am entering a spiritual gasoline station. Here in the station, I can take a rest from my service, obtain enough strength from God, and get back to service.

In April 2003, when Hong Kong was at the peak of the Severe Acute Respiratory Syndrome (SARS) epidemic, I went back there to attend the First Annual Youth Developmental Camp. At the camp, I had the opportunity to share with the young people regarding how missionaries came to China in the late nineteenth and the early twentieth centuries, and how those missionaries offered themselves to God in their youth and let Him use them as He saw fit. I also shared with them how God called me to serve Him.

On the flight to and from Hong Kong, everyone aboard the airplane had to wear a mask. In Hong Kong, no one shook hands, and all I could do was nod at them and pass my greetings to them with my eyes. When I went back to the United States and went to school, everybody at school was afraid of me, treating me like an alien from outer space. They feared that I was contagious. God, however, gave me this opportunity to challenge the young people to rethink their purpose in life, and to consider following the footsteps of our Lord Jesus Christ. I felt my trip to Hong Kong was not wasted at all!

Surprisingly, not three months later, I had another chance to go to Hong Kong. This time I joined the Hong Kong Missionary Kids Caregivers Group to Bangkok, Thailand to run a camp for the missionary kids from Hong Kong. When I was with the children of pastors and missionaries, I recognized my own young shadow in them, just like the story of the ugly duckling who did not know who he was. The duckling put his best effort to intermingle with those who did not know or want to acknowledge him. In the spiritual and worship times at the camp, I encouraged the young people to rethink our heavenly status, which Jesus Christ purchased for us with His precious blood. Since the parents of these youngsters were missionaries, many of had them had lived in various countries and cities. They learned various languages and attended various schools. Even though their status on earth might not be clear, I grasped the opportunity to explain to them that their heavenly status is very clear. Every morning, I led them to use various ways to see how God saw them from His perspective. In the afternoons, the youngsters would have the opportunity to recount their own experiences, come to terms with things, and find strength and support one another.

When I was young, I also experienced changing schools, moving from place to place, and saying goodbye to friends and relatives. These experiences of mine allowed me to understand the feelings of the children of missionaries. Because of this, I could point out the blessings that God has given to them through their trials. Therefore, whenever I have the opportunity to serve children of missionaries, I feel very happy and fulfilled. I also know that I am supported by many prayers of brothers and sisters. These past five years, God has put me in a good school in Los Angeles. I work with good Christian co-workers who encourage and grow with each other. God has also given me opportunities to equip myself further. The biggest joy is to give back to God what belongs to Him. God has also thrown open the floodgates of heaven and poured out so many blessings onto me, just like what Jesus Christ our Lord said, "But seek first His kingdom and His righteousness, and all these things will be given to you as well."

School in the Jungle

After graduating from University and doing internships, I did not know where to find a job. During several interviews, I mentioned I would be going to Papua New Guinea as a student teacher, and several schools expressed interest. However, when I mentioned that I would not be home until the later part of September, they were all silent. I truly believed that God would provide. At the same time, I knew that God would move brothers and sisters to support me with prayers and finances. Therefore I could lay down all worries and step onto the road of short-term missionary work.

The university from which I graduated offers a class which people seldom know about. This class enables students to go abroad as a student teacher on the mission field, and at the same time it is recognized by the Department of Education of the country. Teaching the children of missionaries was the burden and dream God had placed in my heart since I was in high school. In the summer of 2001, I finally arrived in Papua New Guinea to start my first missionary assignment as a teacher. The local weather is good; springtime year-round, with a very long rainy season. Many local people are still living their lives as if they were in the Stone Age. I heard that there are over eight hundred and fifty-three local languages. Most of the languages spoken locally do not have written words. There are no Bibles for the local people to read. The Bible translation foundation had been working there for several years and brought many people to the Lord. They translated the New Testament into one hundred twenty-five tribal languages.

After I arrived in Australia, after two more days of journey on foot and by bus, I finally caught a small airplane. The small airplane passed through valleys, rivers, and forests, and finally it landed in front of the missionary center established by the Bible translation foundation. When I looked at it from the small airplane, it was like a small town. Even though it was shabby, God had provided for everything. It was a small town of two thousand people, one thousand local people, and the rest comprising of missionary teachers, local staff, and students. There were about six hundred missionary children (MKs) in this boarding school in the jungle. Their parents worked and lived in various parts of Papua New Guinea.

The first week at the mission center, I concentrated on preparing my lesson plans and studying the local languages and culture. I tried hard to fit into a new environment and a new way of living. I was tired, both spiritually and physically, and I felt depressed. Small matters were bothering me daily; I felt uncomfortable and blamed them on God and myself. Suddenly I realized I had forgotten the abundant supply of God, and I forgot the calling of

God. I also forgot the purpose for which I came here, to serve people. Friday came at last. At a meeting we shared and prayed for each other. Two of the professors washed our feet to remind us of the goal for which we were here. They exemplified humility and I was touched.

On the weekend before school started, I was taken through mountainous paths to visit a village. The chief and children of the village were eagerly waiting for us to come. They held our hands and guided us to tour their village. We slept in small grass sheds with insects and bugs. Jungle life was such unique experience! We used their language, which we had just learned, to communicate with the local people and to share the gospel with them. I was so overwhelmed by their enthusiastic responses; it preoccupied my mind for a long, long time.

Life in the village was a huge contrast to life in the missionary center. However, life in the missionary center was also shabby compared to the life in a big city. My mind struggled with questions: should missionaries live more comfortably? Do missionaries deserve good or perfect equipment? Should my attitude about missionary life be changed? Why did I donate my old computer to missionary organizations? Shouldn't we offer the best to our Lord Jesus Christ?

After several years of prayer and preparation, this was the time to test the call of God for my life. It was not an issue of pressure, or my ability being tested. Teaching was not my first choice as a profession. However, by His grace, I was able to do well. This was a miracle. This short-term mission of three months went by very quickly. From Monday to Friday, I taught Mathematics; on Saturdays I led the eighth grade student fellowship; and on Sundays I joined the worship service, which combined nineteen nationalities into one huge service. In the circle of missionaries, there were different necessities. Miraculously, God gave different callings and different talents to different people, who formed a harmonious United Nations Army used by Jesus Christ. We were different parts of a united body whose head was Jesus Christ. Praise God! He gave me opportunities to run with everybody towards the same goal. I truly enjoyed the assignments and the interactions.

"Even though I walk through the valley of the shadow of death, I will fear no evil for you are with me." I knew brothers and sisters were praying for me. One time we met some robbers. There were six of them, with guns and knives, who tried to stop our small truck. God listened to our urgent prayers, and we did not lose anything. However, this event reminded me to pray for the lives and safety of missionaries. The next morning we read about the 9/11 incident in the United States. This incident led us to feel that: "Unless the LORD builds the house, its builders labor in vain. Unless the LORD watches over the city, the watchmen stand guard in vain."

Aaron Lee was born in Taiwan to a pastor's family, and followed his parents to Hong Kong at a young age. Aaron speaks Mandarin at home and Cantonese in school like a local. He studied Education at BIOLA and has been teaching high school in Los Angeles since 2001. Aaron has a burden to serve children of missionaries.

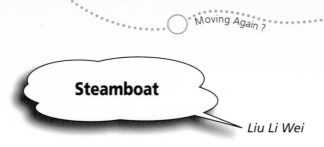

Steamboat

Liu Li Wei

Hello, everybody! I am a junior at Tunghai University, Taiwan, majoring in Fine Arts. My name is Liu Li Wei. I am a MK (missionary kid) who has lived in Thailand, which is famous for steamboats. My life is somewhat like a pot of hot soup with lots of ingredients mixed in it. I grew up in many cultures. I consider myself to be a standard multicultural missionary kid.

When I was very young, one day after children's service, the preacher asked, "Who would like to trust in Jesus Christ?" I raised my hand and said, "I would like to trust in Jesus Christ." Jesus Christ is very special and precious to me.

When I was in kindergarten, my father studied theology in Hong Kong. I have beautiful memories of Hong Kong. When I was in fifth grade, my parents felt that God was leading them to Chiangmai, Thailand to be missionaries. They asked me how I felt about it. Then, the three of us prayed together. They brought me, a ten-year-old child, with them to Chiangmai to seek the guidance of God. To me, this was very abstract. I asked my mother, "Why hasn't God led us to Hong Kong to be missionaries?" However, God was humorous. When my father asked me what I thought of Chiangmai, God allowed me to think about Minnesota where our family went to visit my uncle. The scenery and street decorations in Minnesota were similar to those in Chiangmai, very beautiful. This was how God eradicated the fears in my heart. Actually, I had already forgotten about this incident. Later on, my father reminded me about it. Because of my childlike answer, my parents were clearer about the guidance of God, and followed His lead.

Together, we moved to Chiangmai, Thailand, to a beautiful small town between the cities and the countryside. I enrolled in an international school where I had to learn English and Thai at the same time, which was very difficult for me. Even though my father also had a difficult time learning Thai, he spent time coaching me in English and helping me with my homework. My parents also bought me an expensive electronic dictionary to help me study. The first year was very difficult, and I ended up repeating my fifth grade. For a long time, I felt like a dummy. I would always forget or not understand the reports and assignments given by the teachers. I also misunderstood what people said and entered the wrong classroom. My parents knew that I was quite stressed.

The school's requirement of Thai language standard was not high. I spent three years learning English as a second language. In that school, I finished my elementary education and my first year of high school. In the second year of high school, I went to a new school for the children of missionaries called Grace International School. Since I just passed my English as a Second Language examination, I was the first graduating class of the new school. I spent the rest of my high school years in this school. I familiarized myself with the Thai culture and immersed myself with the local environment. In this international school for children of missionaries, I studied with students from many nations for three years.

The academic life at Grace Academy was very pleasant. Since I was shy, I found it difficult to speak English with those schoolmates whose mother tongue was English. But God allowed me have classmates from Germany, Switzerland, Korea, Japan, and Hawaii. We played basketball together and grew in our band together. I was the only Chinese, and therefore everybody in the school knew who I was. Every year we played basketball in the inter-school league for all Thailand high schools, and I was a member of our school's basketball team. When I entered the game to play, the foreign students of our school would cheer for me, by shouting, "Levi, Levi." Though I was not as strong as other foreign students, my three pointers were deadly. The team coach would send me in at critical moments to win the ball game.

During our last year, most classmates were studying for the United States Scholastic Aptitude Test and applying for universities in the United States of America. Some made plans to go back to their own country for university education; and a few wanted to stay in Thailand for further education. At that time, I was also thinking about my university education, but where? Several universities in the United States of America wrote to me, welcoming me to study there. But I had doubts and fears. I prayed to the Lord Jesus Christ whom I had trusted in since I was a child, and yet I did not know Him much. I tried to ask for His guidance. God gave me a passage from the Bible as His response. In Proverbs chapter three verses five and six, it says, "Trust in the Lord with all your heart and lean not on your own understanding; in all your ways acknowledge Him, and He will make your paths straight." There was still one more year before I was to graduate from high school. I finally made a decision to go back to Taiwan for my university education. This was not easy, because at that time, I had already left the Chinese educational system for seven years. The Chinese I retained was from reading Chinese martial arts novels. My Chinese level made it very difficult for me to prepare myself for the university entrance examinations in Taiwan.

I had to put my trust in Jesus Christ when I prepared to return to Taiwan for my university education. I felt an ease when I trusted Jesus Christ, which I could not find in any other way. On important decisions, I asked Jesus Christ for His opinion. I deeply believed that Jesus Christ was directing me in the roads ahead. I would go where He led me. My soul was set free! I spent my senior year studying for the Taiwan exam, and I experienced the trustworthiness of our Lord. I began to have a deeper relationship with Jesus Christ. I still played basketball and played my instrument in the band. After school everyday, I rode my motorcycle to the food court in a shopping center, searched out a quiet place, and sat down to study because local libraries were already closed at six o'clock in the evening. After eating a simple supper, I studied until nine o'clock and went home to have dinner, which my mother would prepare for me. Now when I think about it, if God had not helped me, I could never have made it through.

Thanks to the Lord for His grace, I was admitted to Tunghai University, Department of Fine Arts. I liked to study fine arts, but I did not have enough confidence. I learned painting in high school from my arts instructor, and that's all. I have never studied under any other artist. Now I am a junior and Fine Arts is not a difficult subject for me after all. There were various tribal groups in Chiangmai, Thailand; and growing up in Chiangmai allowed me to embrace the tribal peoples' beautiful expressions of colors, lines, and forms, with multicultural characteristics. I expressed these freely in my paintings.

What I found more difficult was my adaptation to the Chinese language and culture when I returned to Taiwan for my university education. My official identity was a local student of Taiwan, and therefore I was not given privileges of expatriate Chinese students from other countries. Whether I was at the university or church fellowship, no one considered me a foreign student. At the university, I was a freshman just like everyone else. At first, even I myself did not recognize any differences that I had from the rest.

Not until I was a sophomore at the university did I realize the difficulties I had when I discussed issues with my coworkers at the fellowship. I experienced difficulties in interpersonal relationships and communication. I was really down-hearted. Finally I realized that I had not been in Taiwan for eight years. Even though I made brief trips to Taiwan to attend high school fellowship camps of Campus Crusade, my home was Thailand. I spoke Chinese only to my parents. Some technical or special terms or words were foreign to me. In language ability, I had gone down several rungs. Actually, when I came back to Taiwan when I was a sophomore in high school, I had some embarrassing moments. One time when I was in Taipei taking the Massive Rapid Transit, the people surrounding me spoke languages that I was familiar with; a lot of them were youths like me, however, I did not understand what they were saying. I was so shocked, and for two weeks, I did not dare open my mouth to utter one word. My parents speak fluent Taiwanese, but mine is only "half and half". When an old lady neighbor spoke Taiwanese to me, I could not understand. I smiled, nodded, and uttered, "Yes, yes." She probably thought that this kid could only smile.

While I was in Chiangmai, I was accustomed to a slower pace of life. All of a sudden, I was pushed into the fast-paced university student life of Taiwan. I felt like everything was non-stop. No wonder every summer when I went back to Thailand, my mother thought I was fleeing from a war and coming home to recuperate.

I thank the Lord for His grace in helping me through these three years of my life in Taiwan. I have experienced, "You crown the year with your bounty, and your carts overflow with abundance." He knew my growing up years would become like a 'steamboat', and there must be some deep meaning to it.

_____

Liu Li Wei followed his missionary parents to Thailand when he was in fifth grade. For eight years, he lived and went to school in Chiangmai. When he graduated from high school, it was his clear intention to return to Taiwan for university. Throughout this process, he has experienced God's grace. He is graduating from Tung Hai University majoring in Fine Arts. His parents are with Care Ministries International.

Growing Up On The Move

Mabel Low

I began as a reluctant home owner and gradually grew to love my local Kirkland. Instead of wondering which country I'm in when I wake up in the morning, I cherish the sanctuary and peace of coming back to a quiet and familiar home every single day.

In the first 27 years of my life, I have lived in seven U.S. states, five countries, and have visited a dozen others. I have been drawn towards mobility as other people are drawn towards home. I have a gratefulness for the international experiences that have made me who I am today. One of the benefits is being able to walk into a Russian restaurant and order food in Russian. Another is to turn on the television and say, "Hey, I've been there!" It's funny, but true, that my ears are tuned in to any conversation around me that has anything to do with Russia. I have met people at social gatherings and we felt an instant rapport because of similar language or cultural experiences. One of the funniest connections I have with people from Southeast Asia is durian. Those who dare to taste the fruit inside the spiky green shell often find that the taste, as well as the smell, improves each time they try it. That's how I learned to love durian. For a while, eat.durian was my email address!

After spending a year in Russia, I began working as an interpreter for hospitals in the Seattle area. I was interpreting for Russian, Cantonese and Mandarin speaking patients, helping them to communicate with their doctors and nurses. All my past struggles with language learning turned into moments of deep satisfaction as I helped these people. One day, I walked into the clinic to speak to the receptionist. I told her I was there to interpret for 'Ivan Ivanovich." She said, "Wait a minute. Weren't you here yesterday interpreting Chinese?" I said, "Yes, I sure was," and grinned.

I have friends from India whom I have known since college. Because I used to live in Singapore where there are many Tamil Indians, I could find many things in common to talk about with my Indian friends in college. I studied books about Indian history and even went on a date with an Indian guy.

When I was living in Singapore, my parents directed a cross-cultural training program in which most of the students were Koreans. I was impressed by their dedication to God, intensity of character and committed prayer life. At one time I even wanted to have a Korean boyfriend and to marry a Korean. In college, my friends also included Filipinos and Africans. I joked with friends that I would only date someone who spoke English with an accent.

Growing Up On The Move

I was born in New York City, but whenever I was homesick, it was for Singapore, and later Hong Kong, after my parents moved there. Then after I lived in Russia, there was a homesickness for Russia as well. My Singaporean friend once said, "You must be confused about your identity." I have to admit that he was correct. During all these years, I sought to immerse myself deeply into cultures other than my own American culture.

Growing up on the move, I continually left people behind in every place. As an adult, I wanted to recover some of the loss by giving myself the option of returning to those places and revisiting memories and relationships. Being continually uprooted led to many transient relationships with friends which caused isolation. I could not allow others to trust me, nor could I trust others over a long period of time. Change was always around the corner, so it seemed futile to care deeply about people. In Singapore I did not bond deeply with my peers, and experienced pain as I watched my Singaporean classmates share laughters or tears. I was an observer. The emotional wall around me was observed by my teachers, close friends, and acquaintances, but they thought I was just shy or quiet. I look back and understand that I did this in order to cope.

Maybe I tried to escape from the Singapore school system in which I felt stifled and controlled. It was a girls' school that was very strict. With my parents' permission, I went back to Taiwan to board at Morrison Academy, where my other MK friends from childhood were. Six months into boarding life, I was still crying from homesickness, but I wanted to be responsible for my own decision to leave home. I wanted to face the consequences head on. Boarding school turned out to be some of the most carefree days I have ever known as I relished freedom away from home. I eventually made many friends there. Yet, I still felt the pain of isolation as I held back from being completely vulnerable. I had bonded with friends but not enough to cry at graduation. Months after graduation, I finally wept, as the impact of the relationships I had lost finally hit me. My heart ached to go back in time and bond more deeply with these friends as they had bonded with each other.

Somehow, at 17, I landed back in America. It was time for me to use my childhood memory of this country to negotiate the culture as an adult. I was as good as a foreign student -- Nah, maybe a little better than that. For the next ten years, I felt uneasy at the thought of settling down and would be frequently drawn to any adventure or cause that would take me back on the road. The most deceptive part of my identity crisis was my American accent. No one could tell that I was more foreign than Asian-Americans who spent most of their lives in the States. My words sounded more "American" than who I really was. There were gaps in my knowledge. I had almost zero knowledge of popular music from the 70s and early 80s. I opened my first bank account in college and was completely unaware of the financial system in the U.S. Many of these difficulties were silent and unknown to the people around me. As if my oddness was not accentuated enough, I attended an Asian American church where college kids my age were fairly wealthy and drove new cars. I did not. I didn't care for symbols of middle class American wealth, whether it was suburbia, economic status, materialism, or new cars. I became more and more drawn toward people and groups who were outsiders in America: international students, economically underprivileged, ethnic minorities, the down and out.

One teacher who influenced me was a deconstructionist. He taught me to ideologically tear apart everything that was hierarchical and power controlled. I began to mentally deconstruct everything in my life and became very disillusioned in the process with anything that was established and organized. Incidentally, that professor was black-listed by my conservative Christian university.

After university, I worked at the South China Morning Post in Hong Kong for a little while until my visa could not be extended there. Upon returning to Los Angeles, I began working at the Los Angeles Times. All the while, I was itching to go overseas. So in 1997, I spent a year in Russia tutoring two MKs. Traveling and crossing cultures was my constant. Russia would be the ultimate in the foreign and exotic. My year in

Russia was not easy. I sacrificed a lot to be there. I was tremendously lonely and isolated. It was there that I became more aware of my pain. Eventually, I roughed it out long enough in Russia to realize that life was probably better back in the States. On the night before I left Russia, I wept as I realized that much of my childhood hurt had been brought back to the surface by ministering to these MKs. Processing the pain as an adult was necessary and cathartic.

Overcoming the Fear of Settling Down

Some people have a fear of change and moving. I had a fear of settling down. When Andrew and I were engaged in 1999, there were months of deep soul searching to decide if I was ready for the prospect of spending most of the rest of my life in the U.S.. I spent hours and hours grieving my loss of permanent wandering, knowing that part of me would be left behind in various countries. My identity had been so tied in with being international and moving around, and my parents were still serving in Asia. The pending marriage was the beginning of a farewell to many things that had defined and comforted me, such as moving and the ability to move. Yet, I knew I was marrying someone who has a deep love and respect for my strong cross-cultural opinions.

Andrew is a handsome Chinese all-American softball and basketball player. I find him to be that rare individual who would be observant enough to see through my layers of pretenses and toughness and be bold enough to tell me. I was impressed by his intelligence and loving persistence. Oh yes, he taught me how to balance my check book. Significantly, Andrew represents many of the values that I had resisted in college: he is an all-American Asian. I confessed to him my bitterness toward Asian Americans because I felt like such an outsider among them. Andrew remained steadfast and loyal to me.

I was astounded by his unconditional love for me. I knew that through him, good things were going to come to my life.

Home in Kirkland

We settled in the great American Pacific Northwest. I began as a reluctant home owner and gradually grew to love my local Kirkland. Instead of wondering which country I'm in when I wake up in the morning, I cherish the sanctuary and peace of coming back to a quiet and familiar home every single day. Kirkland knows me: I unexpectedly run into friends at the supermarket, mall, park, etc. Now I have a history with this place and its people: I have continuity, routine and structure.

Our daughters are age seven and three. Raising children also forces me to get to know our local community. Together with Andrew we have formed friendships and bonded with people. I get to know my daughter's nursery teachers at church and at preschool; every week I drive her to AWANA or to ice skating class. Without immediate family in town, Andrew and I take the initiative to pick up the phone and ask people to babysit for us occasionally. I worked at a local church preschool for two and a half years.

Now I am engaging myself with this culture and people, and absorbing various aspects of Americana. I identify myself with America, for better or for worse. My hobbies include travel (of course), following national politics on CNN and MSNBC, teaching Mandarin to my daughters, and contributing articles to publications from time to time.

My Word to Youths Whose Lives are Transient

Teenagers normally experience awkwardness and transition in exploring their identities. However, being a teenager in many different cultures is even harder. I had different identities in different situations. I could not explain my American self to Singaporean friends, my Singaporean self to American friends, or my Taiwan self to anyone. Even my parents could not fully understand me. I hope this comes close to hearts of the children of refugees, missionaries, military and diplomatic personnel, business people, and immigrants. As children and youths, you are vulnerable and too young to know how to do anything but cope. As you become adults, you will wake up to the reality of how your experiences have influenced you. In a nutshell, often due to immaturity and innocence, walls are built to protect injured emotions. No one fully knew, no one could really be blamed. It was allowed by God although I don't believe He desired the pain.

I wish I could prescribe a formula. All I can say is each person needs to process things at his pace and in God's way. Submit your experiences to the Word of God, such as Ephesians 4 and Philippians 2. Choose scriptures that encourage you, and read them over and over again. I have favorite passages that comfort and motivate me. What you can do is look around at your workplace, your church, your family and friends and give thanks to God for them. These are gifts from God.

I have been blessed to be part of two of the very best churches in Kirkland. My women's Bible study is solid and packed with women who fear God and put the Word of God before how they feel on any given day. "Feelings follow faith." We are women of faith who do not depend on how we feel to tell us what our day is going to be like today. I learned from older women in the church about how to successfully go through the seasons of life. My husband is also very stable and persevering. By the way, he hates moving. What a balance for me! And as good spouses do, he gives me feedback and a secure environment for character growth.

Mabel was born in New York City, and spent her early years between the States and a one-classroom MK school in the small town of Taitung, Taiwan. The middle school years happened in Singapore and the remainder of her high school at Morrison Academy of Taiwan. She married Andrew Low in 1999. The Low family, formerly of Kirkland, Washington, now reside in Irvine, California.

* Part of this article first appeared in Kids Without Borders, OMF and HKACM publishing, Hong Kong, 2000. Rewritten and expanded in 2008.

Love Unspoken

Ruth Lam

"Mark, Mark…" I yelled and turned the corner. "I got a check!" Smiling, he held up the same letter to me. In total, we had US $4000. It was the exact amount we needed for school. God knew…He answered just in the nick of time. Together we walked to the Financial Services Office. It was THE DAY… definitely, the day that the Lord showed us His deep faithfulness.

Who am I?

One of the most challenging questions for an MK is the question, "Where are you from?" With this question, comes, "Who am I?" When I was in second grade, my parents and I moved to live in Singapore as missionaries. We happened to live where there were many foreigners. The previous director who held my dad's new job had the office and his residence in this part of Singapore. Some of our friends in the neighborhood went to the American School. We went to local public school with the national school kids. After school, we would play baseball on the street, or on rainy days, walk in the drains filled with rainwater. One day, two Caucasian kids came over to my gate. We started to play. They asked me where I was from. I told them I was "American." They didn't believe me. They said I was lying. We started a shouting match.

"I am too!"
"Are not!"
"Am too!"

"No, you're not!" The match went on. I had to prove that I was the real authentic thing.

"Wait till I prove it to you!" I shouted. And with that, I raced into my home and asked mom for my US passport.

She questioned me, "Why do you want your passport?"

"I just need it." My mom would not give it to me. Being so flustered, I could not explain why it was so urgent for me to have it. Finally, I raced outside but the girls were gone. I couldn't prove to them who I was. Who was I anyhow?

(Postscript: It is not until coming to know the Lord that the identity situation becomes less painful. I know I am the Lord's child. Reading and learning about the Third Culture Kids' Theory and experience has helped me put labels on who I am. Going to counseling has helped me grieve through events of my childhood and adolescence. I am a Third Culture Kid but also a Third Culture Adult now and I have two MKs of my own. I am OK with not being able to call one place my home. I am alright with the loss and the grief of losing valued friendships and familiar places, because I am a Third Culture person and that is how this life is. The trick is learning how to grieve and put my identity in Jesus)

Enculturation Problems

We didn't have much extra money when I was growing up. And when challenges came, the motto was "Trust in God". When I was in fourth grade, in Singapore, I struggled so much in Chinese class, and that was just the tip of the iceberg. The year and a half or so before moving to Singapore was spent in San Rafael, California, in a little sleepy town as my mom and dad furthered their study at Golden Gate Seminary. Mom and Dad tried to speak to my brother and me in Chinese while we were on furlough, but we were reluctant participants. We were Americans, not Chinese. So, my brother and I really lost a lot of our Chinese language when we stayed in America for that period of time. When we went to Singapore again for the second time, I had a hard time in Chinese class. My parents didn't have extra money for tutoring. Everybody in Singapore had tutors, so it seemed, but we didn't. Mom helped us the best she could, but it was a big struggle.

The struggle continued for the next 3 years. However, my recollection only becomes clearer when I was in 7th grade (Secondary 1). I was a very good student. I worked hard but no amount of working made me feel comfortable in Chinese class. When Wang Lao She (Teacher Wang) called me to read aloud, I would cringe inside. My palms would get sweaty and I stumbled through the words on the page. My sympathetic friend sitting behind me would whisper me the words I couldn't read. It was such a hopeless feeling, that I think the teacher even gave up asking me questions or making me read. Once when we had a substitute, the teacher asked me to read and the whole class said, "Teacher, she can't read. Don't ask her." I looked like everyone else, but inside, I was not all Chinese, especially not Singaporean Chinese.

However, my dad and mom said, "Its OK. Just do your best and trust." I trusted God, but I felt terrible inside about my Chinese. I felt stupid for struggling so much. Ironically, God has called me back to a Chinese-speaking place. He has redeemed a lot of my childhood pain. My Chinese is still not that great!

Not Enough Closure

Faith was a big thing in my family. Talking openly, especially about negative things or uncomfortable things, wasn't done in a very healthy manner. When I was a child, from the time I was 2 to 15, I lived in 10 different places and three geographic locations in the world.

I remember it was summer school in 1979. We were in San Rafael. My mom and dad had enrolled my brother and I in summer school. I did gymnastics. That was so fun. All my friends like Nikki, Alexander and Alice were all there. On the last day of summer school, my mom drove me to Alice's apartment complex. I gave her my blue bike with the silver handlebars. We had a station wagon then, and the back of it was all packed with our belongings. We were leaving. I don't remember packing up our stuff or talking about it. I don't remember mom and dad dealing with the sadness and grief of leaving. It was just something we did, and we just packed and left. There weren't many words that were spoken to each other about the loss. If I did talk about it, dad and mom would negate the sad feelings and say that we would be okay. At least we were together. However, I remember the tears staining my face as I waved goodbye to Alice, who stood at the curb with my blue bicycle.

Inadequate closure brings much grief and negative coping patterns. My parents are western in many ways. They are not traditional or stereotypical Chinese parents who expect you to be high achievers or have good professions. They just expect us to do our best, love and follow the Lord. They are however, quite Chinese, when it comes to emotions and the communicating of hard emotions.

When I was fifteen, a few months shy of sixteen, mom and dad dropped me off at my grandmother and my aunt's home in Massachusetts. I was going to go to 12th grade and live in America. I was excited but didn't foresee the pain that would come with separation from my parents. Though we moved a lot as a family, we were always together. I took for granted what that was like. I did well in Singapore but the school system was very rigid. There were not many choices. I was a good student and tracked in the Pure Arts stream, studying subjects like Literature and History. There was no chance to study Computer or anything different in your stream. So, together with mom and dad, we decided that it was better for me to go back to America.

On a snowy first day of school, I was going to attend Newton North High school, a few blocks from my aunt's home. My mom and dad had to leave. They had to catch a flight to some city where Dad was preaching. The snow fell hard that day. Through the window, and through my tears, I saw the flakes fluttering down. My dad didn't say much. He just said he loved me and was proud of me.

Before that day, we didn't talk about how hard it would be to leave each other. We never discussed why life was like this or why they couldn't stay in America for a while. We didn't express the sadness in words of missing each other. I didn't dare ask dad to stay because I knew he couldn't. There were meetings, schedules to keep; he was on the deputation trail. All the unspoken questions I had, laid dormant in my mind. So, I left for school as they hopped into the car to go to the airport.

I mustered up all my courage to walk into that school building. There were kids all over; black, white, very tall, very big, very loud. I willed myself to stop crying and just make it. Just find the classes and go to school. Don't think about the pain of not seeing mom and dad for a long time. Don't think about missing them. Block out the screaming voice that says,

"Why can't it be different?" I walked to my assigned locker and tried to open the door. As hard as I tried, I couldn't get it to open. I never saw a locker in real life, only in the movies. Finally, after several minutes of pulling and pushing and biting my lips to avoid the despair that filled my heart, I spoke to a very tall brown-haired boy next to me. "Could you open this for me?" The look on his face revealed the disbelief he had that someone would not know how to open a locker. "Click" went the locker and the door opened. I muttered "thanks" and that began my life in America. It also ended for me the reality that our family was going to be together in one place at one time.

God is Faithful

As a sophomore at Biola University, one of the most stressful times for me was "Pay Day" at the Financial Services office. My brother Mark was also at Biola and he was a junior. In order to attend Biola, my brother worked two jobs and took a part-time load so he would not have to take out a loan. I had a partial scholarship, took out a small student loan and worked to get some money to pay the school tuition. Since we did not have enough money to pay the full semester cost of the tuition up front, we would pay in installments.

It was the fourteen of the month. They next day was the dreaded day to hand in tuition funds at the Financial Services Office. Mark and I sat at the cafeteria discussing our plan of action to face the Financial Service office. "We'll just have to tell them we don't have the money," Mark reasoned. "Will they let us pay a little bit?" I questioned. We decided the only thing we could do was pray. "Lord, you know our needs. We can't come up with $4000 today. Please help us." After talking it through, Mark and I decided to go to the office after chapel the next day.

Students streamed out of the gym on the fifteenth of that month. It was THE DAY and we didn't have the money. Passing by the post office where we would collect our personal mail, Mark and I went to check our mailboxes. His box was around the corner from mine. Putting the key into the slot, I opened the box. "Junk mail, junk mail; hey, what's this?" It was a letter from North Carolina, Westover Church. I quickly tore the envelope open.

"Dear Ruth,

This Christmas, our church took up a special offering for all the MKs we support. The offering total was _____ and we have divided this equally among all the children of our missionaries. Enclosed is a check for $2000. Have a good year at school."

"Mark, Mark...!" I yelled and turned the corner. "I got a check!" Smiling, he held up the same letter to me. In total, we had US $4000. It was the exact amount we needed for school. God knew...He answered just in the nick of time. Together we walked to the Financial Services Office. It was THE DAY...definitely, the day that the Lord showed us His deep faithfulness.

Ruth Lam張嫻光 and her husband Peter林振光 are currently ministering as poverty relief workers sent to East Asia as missionaries with the First Evangelical Church Association. Ruth was born to missionary parents and lived in three different countries during her childhood and youth. Vowing never to become a missionary herself, she encountered the quiet call of God during her junior year in University. In 1999, Ruth and Peter along with their daughter Kaitlin Emily abandoned the American dream of good jobs and financial security in obedience to the Lord's calling to serve the poor and the unreached in East Asia. Being a MK and TCK, Ruth is familiar with transition and loss as well as the gifts of grace from God to learn to love another culture, cultivate trust, and be surprised each day with the lessons the Lord teaches her as she serves others in a cross-cultural setting. She has a deep compassion for MKs on the field and finds it a privilege to walk alongside her daughters, Kaitlin Emily林文詩 (9) and Analynn Joy林恩詩(2) and other MKs in her field of ministry.

Did You Eat Cheese in Taiwan?

Linda Feldman

I decided early on to not get offended by these questions, "Did you eat cheese in Taiwan?" After all, people were unknowingly exposing themselves, making themselves vulnerable by showing their own ignorance. Be kind, I told myself, but sometimes, I found it really, really hard.

I grew up in Taipei, Taiwan. My dad was a missionary pastor and my mom was a missionary wife. "Wo mama shr mei gwo ren, baba shr chung gwo ren (My mother is American and my dad is Chinese)." I would often use these words when out in public with my friends. The street vendor that I was buying a watch from or the woman who made my shaved-ice milk dessert would ask without hesitation, "Are you American?" It never bothered me. In one glance, Chinese people can tell that I'm not completely Chinese. Sometimes they can't see the Chinese at all. This always baffles white Americans who can seemingly only see the Chinese side of me. I later learned in a sociology class that there is a term for this phenomenon: the rule of hypo descent, that if a person is part minority, then they will be seen as part of the minority group, even if they are equally part of the majority.

I am exactly one half Chinese and one half white, yet when I was going to college in largely white West Michigan, dorm dinner conversations would often turn to my overseas upbringing. "Did you eat cheese in Taiwan?" I did notice that my white missionary kid friends were not inundated with these questions. Why? White Americans around the world eat cheese, of course. It doesn't matter where they live. I decided early on to not get offended by these questions. After all, people were unknowingly exposing themselves, making themselves vulnerable by showing their own ignorance. Be kind, I told myself, but sometimes, I found it really, really hard. My husband tells me I have a knack for making other people uncomfortable. He calls it my gift. It's hard to control your gift, you know. Try, I do, but sometimes my "gift" gets the better of my friends and I...

"You remind me of someone," Brooke said. "I couldn't put my finger on who it was until just now! Do you know Lucy Lui from Ally McBeal?

I actually knew whom she was talking about. There were only three or four recognizable Asian-American actresses on the scene at that time – Lucy Lui being one of them. She's beautiful, but have I ever thought I looked remotely like her? No.

"You're just saying that 'cuz I'm Asian, aren't you?" I said, laughing. Her smile fading, a look of discomfort came across her face, and she went pale. Oops. "I'm just kidding. Isn't she in that movie Charlie's Angels?" The conversation, thankfully, moved on.

Matt and I got engaged when I was in graduate school. He was in graduate school a hundred miles away, so many of my classmates had never met him. The first question I got when I told them we were engaged was, "Is he Chinese?" This caught me off guard. There was no response to be had, although I often wondered if my black friends were asked similar questions. I doubt it. There seems to be a special sensitivity sometimes bordering on nervousness given to Blacks by Whites in America. A sensitivity that is much more lax toward Asians. It doesn't bother me, as long as I can use these situations as a tool to show people their biases with my gift. After some thought, I came up with a response that I was able to use several times: "No," I'd say, "He's White, like you."

Accent

I have been told that I have a Chinese accent, although English is my first language and I do NOT have an accent. Of course, I take advantage of some people...I convinced several people that I was a martial arts expert, without having ever taken lessons. Another time, at Calvin, there was a bulletin board up in one of the dorms that had pictures of starving children in 3rd world countries. I told the friend that I was with, "No way. I can't believe they put my cousin's picture up here!" Sadly, he believed me and never trusted me again.

I found out when I was a teen that my Uncle Bill tried to keep my mom from marrying my dad. He was a pastor at the time, a graduate of Bob Jones University. One of his arguments would be why my parents should get married? He said that it was unnatural, that the children would be deformed. Well, here I am, Uncle Bill! I AM deformed! I have this gift – the gift of making people uncomfortable. :o)

Linda grew up as a missionary kid in Taipei, Taiwan. She worked for a time as an occupational therapist, but currently homeschools her 3 sons and has a small, home-based sewing pattern company. Linda and Matt Feldman with their 3 children reside in Texas.

An Outsider By Choice

— Elaine Chen Persson

I think what I need to realize as a parent is that TCKs can never feel a sense of belonging except with other TCKs. At the same time, I must allow my children to participate in the decision-making process of moving overseas. If they also own that "higher calling," they will be better able to deal with the isolation. They will know that God called them and that God has a purpose for them living overseas.

I believe my childhood can be split into two phases: pre-sixth grade and post-sixth grade. Before sixth grade, I lived in confusion and loneliness, and after sixth grade, I found a sense of belonging. What made the difference? For that, I must talk about my childhood experiences from the lens of a TCK.

At the age of two, my family moved from Taiwan (where I was born) to the U.S.. I have no memory of Taiwan before we moved to the States, so I feel that my life began in the U.S.. Of course, those were the pre-school years and I lived my carefree life playing with mom and dad, and my other toddler friends. I remember church and Sunday School. I remember not understanding English and I remember understanding English. I remember going to preschool. When I turned four, we moved back to Taiwan.

From age four to eight, we lived in Taiwan. Those were also the years I began my formal education. I was definitely not a well-adjusted child or student in Taiwan. I did not flourish, I survived. I remember always being confused at why my teachers were always angry with me, and why I was always getting punished. I'm not sure if my confusion was due to being a TCK (was I already a TCK by then?) or merely from my personality? But whatever it was, I remember confusion and I remember isolation, especially in school.

When I was eight, our family moved back to the States once again. I had forgotten all my English by then, and I was placed in ESL for two years. We moved to Thousand Oaks, California, a city that was at that time predominately caucasian. There were very few Third Culture Kids there. Those who were TCKs like me were ashamed and tried our best to acculturate. But no matter how good our English became, we knew that we were different. I was so desperate to fit in that I told some girls about a boy I had a crush on. After that, I was utterly embarrassed. I had forced myself to do something that was very "American," but that was totally outside of my Chinese culture. After I attempted such a brave act to belong to "them," I felt even more isolated. How can anyone ever truly belong when the actions they do, to be part of the group, betray who they really are? I knew I was a fake, even though I was only in fourth and fifth grade. I felt trapped. Will I always feel like an outsider? I wondered.

Then came sixth grade. We moved once again. This time, we moved to Pasadena, California, and my world changed. I moved from a mostly non-immigrant city to a city where only two people in my class were caucasian. There I met my two best friends, Patricia and Maria. Both were Mexican Americans. Both were TCKs. What was different about them was that they spoke Spanish constantly, not only to their parents who couldn't speak English, but sometimes they would choose to speak Spanish instead of English to each other! They actually liked the "Mexican" part of their

Mexican American heritage. That was an eye-opener for me. I was trying to erase the "Chinese" part of me, when all along, I needed to first understand that I am not Chinese and I am definitely not American, I am Chinese American. A third kind of culture.

Because so many of us in Pasadena, California were this third kind of culture, we huddled together, and we found community with one another. We belonged to each other. Without being conscious of it, after we moved to Pasadena, my friends became exclusively other TCKs. Kids are drawn to make friends with whom they get along with, and not surprisingly, I was drawn to other TCKs because it was only with them that I felt a true sense of belonging. I was keenly aware when I would leave my third culture environment, because alienation always resulted; no matter if it was with other Chinese people (as we moved back to Taiwan once again when I turned 14,) or when I chose to join a non-third culture Christian fellowship in college. I think I was lucky to have grown up among other TCKs. Instead of being lost and trying desperately to fit into the culture of residence, I actually had my own community, which not many TCKs find outside of large immigration populations like Los Angeles. We would go to school dances and football games AND we would drink boba milk and eat gluttonous rice with sweetened red beans. We were definitely our own culture.

My life changed drastically when I decided to move away from Los Angeles and to go into full-time missions. On January 1998, I traveled to Scotland to do a Discipleship Training School with Youth With a Mission. Even though I lived in Los Angeles and had been exposed to many different cultures, my worldview was very Chinese/Asian mixed with mainstream west coast American culture. But moving to Scotland exposed me to the European cultures. Not just that, I was exposed to the European Christian culture, which was very different from Chinese American Christian culture. I loved it, because I experienced the bigger picture of what God's people and God's character are like. It was wonderful. I continue to serve with Youth With A Mission today.

I met my husband in the fall of 1998. He was also serving full-time and we met during a training school. He moved from Sweden to the U.S. at the age of 20. We were classmates, then friends, and a year and half later, we were married. I have only good things to say about cross-cultural marriages. Just as individuals are imperfect, every culture has godly parts but also has its shortcomings. Being married to a person of a different culture prevents us from becoming blinded to the shortcomings of our own culture. It brings to light both the good and the bad. As everything is brought into the light, we can examine and discuss the differences and expose the godly as well as the ungodly. I truly believe that we have become more Kingdom-like as a result. God puts a little imprint of His character in every culture. Being married to someone who is neither Asian nor American has helped me to see more of God's character. I also believe that our daughter will benefit the most from this cross-cultural marriage, because she will be raised up in two cultures and will receive the benefit of both. Hopefully, she will see our loving God from both an Asian perspective and from a Scandinavian perspective. That is wonderful. We all need to know our loving God more.

As a married adult, I am once again living outside of my familiar Chinese American community. However, this time, it's my choice, and I'm following a "higher calling." My husband is Swedish and our daughter, who is four, will grow up speaking not only English, but Swedish and Chinese as well. I don't know what her childhood will be like, but she will most likely grow up as a TCK since we expect to live overseas (not America) in the future. I think what I need to realize as a parent is that TCKs can never feel a sense of belonging except with other TCKs. At the same time, I must allow my children to participate in the decision-making process of moving overseas. If they also own that "higher calling," they will be better able to deal with the isolation. They will know that God called them and that God has a purpose for them living overseas.

Elaine Chen Persson grew up in a missionary family. Her dad serves as a mission leader based in Taiwan, also traveling to other mission fields. They currently reside in Colorado Springs serving in a mission organization that focuses on the unreached in the 10/40 Window. They served among the minorities in East Asia for a number of years and continue to travel to the field on a regular basis.

Working in Hong Kong

— Joshua Chan

I just finished my last day of work in Hong Kong. In a few weeks, job hunting and part-time studying will start elsewhere again in Canada. Although it has only been just one year of working and living in Hong Kong after graduating from university, reflecting on this period reveals many difficulties and blessings that have come as a result of staying in this city.

I was born in Hong Kong and at the age of three, my family moved to Japan because of my parents' decision to become Christian missionaries.

I went to a local Japanese kindergarten and then an international boarding school for primary school with my older brother. While studying at Chefoo School, we only got to see our parents three times a year during the holidays.

Even though it was hard at the beginning, we soon forgot about our worries and started enjoying the freedom with the other students in the new environment! Amidst all these changes, we became used to moving around to different locations each year.

After nine long memorable years of living in Japan, my parents finished their time there and we headed back to Hong Kong. To call the first year back in Hong Kong a culture shock would be an understatement!

I remember vividly one time when it was the first day in Chinese history class and I had forgotten my textbook. The teacher found out that I did not have my textbook. She singled me out in front of the whole class, and asked a lot of questions that I did not understand. I started crying. It was only after my classmates told her that I grew up in Japan that she allowed me to sit down! Thankfully, I do not remember the classes when the teacher lectured on the not so pleasant history between China and Japan!

Two years later, just when I thought I had settled into Hong Kong life, my parents found new job opportunities in Toronto, Canada. We all moved yet again. I thought studying and living in Canada would be similar to the American and British schooling system. I was familiar with those systems in Japan. In some sense it was. Many people thought that I was a normal Canadian Born Chinese (CBC). But after explaining my background, people usually became even more confused.

For my post-secondary education, I decided to stay in Canada because my family was there. In the end, I got accepted into the computer science program at the University of Waterloo. Being on campus, I enjoyed being able to interact with international students. I got involved with the Japanese club and exchange students.

The computer program was five years long and mid-way through it, I realized that I just could not stay in one place for such a long period of time. So, I decided to do a student exchange program in Germany. I felt like I just had to move on. With a year of basic German language under my belt, I tried to immerse myself into the culture by studying and working there for the whole year. It turned out to be a really unique experience, being in contact with so many cultures in Europe. I was able to have the opportunity to travel and to see many diverse lifestyles of the local populations. After spending my time there, it is fair enough to say that doors that I never knew existed have been opened. The idea of living there again sometime in the future would not be out of the question.

After returning to Canada, I somehow managed to graduate on time. Not being able to find a job in Toronto straight away, I decided to take a prolonged graduation trip with my brother by traveling from Germany to Hong Kong by land. The visit to Hong Kong was intended to merely be a destination point to visit all the relatives and friends again before returning to Canada. It could not have turned out to be more different.

Born in Hong Kong but reared in Japan, I had never seriously considered Hong Kong as a place to live or work if I had the choice. To me, it was more of a place where the family would buy inexpensive items, eat from a large selection of ridiculously delicious Chinese food, and meet relatives and church friends. Even in the two school years that I studied in Hong Kong, I felt quite out of place having to speak with my limited Cantonese and hang out with friends who had totally different interests.

So when friends and family found out that I decided to work in HK, they were needless to say somewhat surprised. The plan was to head back but after realizing that there were a lot of good reasons to stay, I decided to do just that. My cousin's wedding was in a few months; friends and relatives kept on encouraging and persuading me to stay. There was a curiosity inside of me to see how living and working full-time in Hong Kong would be like. My grandpa, one time before I left for Japan, said that I needed to remember that I was Chinese, not Japanese. There was something about the challenge of wanting to change my own unsatisfactory perception of Hong Kong, especially when I called myself Chinese.

Applying to different positions in Hong Kong was a bit harder than I thought. Depending on the position, there were different levels of Chinese reading and writing abilities required. All the positions that I found, required the ability to speak Cantonese but the local companies usually also expected one to read and write Chinese.

My parents tried to give me Chinese reading and writing lessons at an early age. But like many Chinese kids living outside Hong Kong, I tried to avoid it at all costs. That naturally led to my substandard Chinese reading and writing skills later on, which I still regret to this day. On the other hand, one thing that I have been quite grateful for is my parents' decision to keep speaking Cantonese in the family even though my brother and I were in Japan. There, we heard Japanese spoken daily and English was used in our international schools.

Despite this language inadequacy, I was able to find a suitable software developer position that matched my qualifications. It was at a relatively small web development company primarily designing and creating websites. Whenever there was anything in Chinese that I did not understand, I inquired of my colleagues who, thankfully, were very understanding. Unlike many international or larger companies in Hong Kong, none of my colleagues knew how to speak English. This posed a huge challenge toward making any meaningful connections with them. It forced me to speak up more and talk about things that they could relate to. Sometimes it was quite frustrating at lunch time when all my colleagues talked about things like Cantonese popular music (Cantopop), local pop stars, and nightly TV shows. All these topics were new to me! Other more enjoyable moments included times when we noticed and shared about the cultural differences in values and practices between Hong Kong and countries like Japan, Canada, or Germany. There is one particular activity the whole office did which I sorely miss. Every Friday, we had afternoon tea together. It is only in Hong Kong that I would eat so much on Fridays at work!

Outside of work, I recognized the need to have English-speaking friends as well to keep myself sane and connected with a group. At the beginning, I felt rather forlorn living in a new city. It took some time but perseverance paid off in the long run. By joining numerous events like church fellowships and weekly soccer games, I was able to meet a lot of new people.

Looking back, there were times where I earnestly thought it was a waste of time trying to deal with all the frustrations involved with being back in my home country that I did not grow up in. Now, I can honestly say that it was well worth it. As I head back to Canada, I'll be taking away with me many pleasant memories. My hope is that others who do stay in Hong Kong will also be able to adjust well and enjoy Hong Kong for what it truly is.

_____

Joshua Chan was born in Hong Kong and grew up in Japan as an MK. He later graduated from the University of Waterloo, Canada, with a degree in Computer Science. Playing soccer and traveling are his main passions and he hopes to continue studying International Development in the near future.

On Being Bicultural

Florence On

Nowadays, it is not unusual to see mixed racial couples and their offspring on the streets of the cities of North America. Usually not even a glance is thrown their way, unless it is to admire their unusually good-looking children. In fact, now, marrying interracially may not necessarily imply a bicultural union as well, because often the man and woman, if they are 2nd or 3rd generation North Americans, share the same cultural heritage, even if not the same skin color. That was not the case when I was born.

My father was a new Cantonese Chinese immigrant to the U.S., my mother from a 1st generation Spanish family in New York. So I was not only of mixed race but also bicultural, and in those days, at the end of WWII, a so-called "half-breed". Many states including Virginia didn't allow interracial marriages, and even in urban northeast U.S., it was difficult. Both my parents were baptized Christians, but had to search before finding a minister who was willing to marry a mixed racial couple. None of my mother's family attended the wedding. There were only 6 guests including the best man and the bridesmaid.

My father was the dominant cultural influence in our home, especially when we lived in New York City near his relatives in Chinatown. We would meet our "Uncles and Aunties" for Noodles or Dim Sum every Sunday after church. My father taught us to respect and obey our elders, our teachers, the importance of education, doing well in school, and of course family was most important. I, as the eldest child, was expected to set a good example to my younger siblings, and if they misbehaved, it was also my fault. He often instructed us with Confucian sayings. Since he was a great cook, we had Chinese meals (3 dishes and soup) for supper, and all of us children used chopsticks since age 3 or 4. We were discouraged from talking during meals as my father wanted the quietness to appreciate the food, and maybe also felt that children's chatter was not proper, as he had been taught at home in China. Sometimes I longed to have warm conversations at meals like my American friends. Discipline was harsh.

My mother was responsible for our spiritual upbringing. She made sure we went to church and Sunday school. She read the Bible and prayed with us every evening, and helped us memorize many Psalms. She also encouraged us to read books and took us to the library weekly until we were old enough to walk there by ourselves.

I was the first of 5 children born over a period of 14 years, and maybe the difficulties of being both of mixed race and bicultural were more pronounced in the 50s and early 60s. We looked more Chinese as toddlers and young children. My teachers were kind for the most part, though there were a few specific episodes of racism in 3rd grade elementary school when a teacher discriminated against myself and a boy from Eastern Europe. Once, I was not feeling well and told her. She put me in the coat closet for a while, thinking that I was disobedient. When she took me out I still kept my head on my desk. I was sent off to the principal, who established I had a high fever and sent for my mother. Our doctor diagnosed scarlet fever. (This teacher was later fired for alcoholism and being drunk in school).

My father had a Chinese hand laundry and a Chinese gift shop. Sometimes the neighborhood children would run by the laundry, throwing stones at the window, yelling:

*"Chink Chink Chinaman, sittin' on the fence,
Tryin' to make a dollar out of 15 cents",*

among other epithets. After school we spent most of our time in my father's store doing homework, helping out, serving customers, and delivering laundry etc. Working in my father's store also made me feel so different from other children. However, I remember being comforted in Jr. High because a pretty German/American girl named Ingrid used to walk home from school with me. Her parents owned the German delicatessen across the avenue from our store and they also lived behind their shop, where she and her brothers helped out after school.

My sister, who is 4 years younger than I, and who during her school years never verbalized any dissatisfaction with our upbringing, began, after she was grown and married, to bemoan our underprivileged childhood circumstances, my father's frugality, and his form of discipline, etc. She expressed the lack of affection our father showed us as children. True, when we were toddlers and until we started school, my father would hug us, lift us up on his lap, and play with us, but not after school age. Also, my father never praised us, even when we did well in school, sports, or music. It was always "you can do better". If our grades were B+'s we were to get A's. If A's, then we were to get A+'s. He was distant and feared. My sister felt that my father favored my brother (who was 11 months younger than I). I never thought that to be the case. If anything, my brother bore the brunt of harsh discipline and sometimes corporal punishment for disobedience or school problems. All of us were encouraged to get higher education, despite the fact that my father only had a Jr. high school education in China. He was most unlike other Chinese of his generation who believed it was a waste to educate girls.

Though Chinese in general don't celebrate the birthdays of children, but only do so beginning the venerable age of 60, it was remarkable that my dad did celebrate our birthdays. (In Taiwan many of my friends, colleagues, my age or younger had never celebrated their birthdays!). He showed his love by cooking for us. We were allowed to choose any dish we wanted for our birthday dinner. My choices were squab and sharks fins soup (the squab ordered in from Chinatown ahead of time by my uncle, the sharks fins from the American neighbors who were hobby fishermen).

Since I had already been to Malaysia and then Taiwan on short term missions trips when my sister started complaining, I remember telling her that in Asia, many Chinese families lived behind or above their shops, the children were expected to help out after school, and were seen running in and out. The lack of expression of outward affection and praise, and the harsh discipline, seemed to me to be common among Chinese fathers. If we had been brought up in Asia, we would have been the norm!

There were many things that troubled me as a mixed race child. Every school year we had to fill out a form and check off whether we belonged to the category: white, or colored. I was never sure what to do. When I was about 8 or 9, our family drove to Virginia to visit a cousin of my Dad's who wanted to sell him his family restaurant. While stopping to eat at a diner, I had to go to the bathroom, but didn't know whether to go to the "White" or "Colored" one. If I went with my mother, I could go to the one with the sign "White". But my mother didn't need to go, and I couldn't explain my distress to her. My Dad was quite interested in buying the restaurant, but a sheriff in the town (friend of my uncle) advised him not to. My uncle and aunt were both Chinese. However, in Virginia mixed race marriages were illegal, and if my father died, my mother would not be considered his legal wife and we would be "bastards", unable to inherit.

For a time I secretly despised my mother in my heart for marrying my Dad and bringing all that turmoil upon me. Now, of course, I am deeply ashamed of these childhood feelings. She was a good mother to me when I was in elementary school and Jr. High, and she herself had many problems adjusting to my dad and his alien culture (and vice-versa). I asked myself why she should marry a Chinese. One day my brother and I were going through my Mom's things and found her High School graduation autograph book. There was one entry by a classmate:

> "Red, blue, yellow and pink
> May you never marry a chink."

My brother and I looked at each other with distress, wondering why my mother didn't heed the warning. We never said another word about it. There were very complicated feelings in my heart, for though I was ashamed of being half Chinese, still, I felt deeply the injustice of my father's inferior social status due to race. I noticed the way sometimes his customers, the church people, and my mother's friends ignored or looked down on him or her.

As my features grew less Asian, I wanted to hide my origins, but it was impossible because of the association with my father's Chinese laundry. I had numerous clashes with my parents because I didn't want to work in the front of the store and be seen by customers; there was seldom work in the back of the store for us children except in the evening. My parents thought I was lazy and I could never bring myself to explain to them the real reason. I just wanted to be like everyone else and not be "different", which I later found to be the cherished desire of many immigrant or bicultural children.

All throughout my school years, I was very quiet and shy, and lacked the self-confidence of typical American students, and although I did participate in some intramural sports and other school activities, I never felt like "part of the gang", but always like an outsider. I didn't know how to "let go", to crack jokes, and I didn't understand the typical humor of Americans.

In college, things changed. Though still a quiet and shy person, I made my first real friendships and belonged to a clique of academically minded students, who were fun and outgoing and loved music. The small college I attended was quite monoethnic: there were only 2-3 blacks and 1-2 students of Asian background, but none of them were in my class. Separated from the stigma of my father's Chinese hand laundry, I simply ignored the Chinese part of myself and my non-typical background seemed to concern no one else. Even when I attended Harvard Graduate School to obtain my Masters degree in language and literature, I lived in a very mono-ethnic dorm and never befriended any Asian Americans. It was a time of my life when the Chinese part of me was dormant. I concentrated on my Spanish/European heritage. It was at that time that I became a Christian and was influenced greatly by thinking Christian Americans who had been brought up in Europe and were also "different".

At this point I want to explain why I rebelled completely against Christianity, secretly during my H.S. years and overtly during my college years. I didn't become a Christian until I was 21. In my childhood, I noted that many of the people in the large monoethnic churches, which we attended from my 4th grade onwards, didn't accept my father. They practically ignored him for the most part. He must have felt strange…my mother would linger on to talk with friends after the service, and my Dad and I would walk home immediately. In my Jr. High years, he began to attend the evening service instead, and I went with him. We would sit in the back, and were the first to leave, in order to avoid any uncomfortable social rebuffs. Later (when I was in college) my parents found a small church where there were several races represented, and he felt at home. The hypocrisy of Christians unsettled me, particularly regarding racism. There were many churches that still preached that marrying a person of another race was against God's will.

One of my roommates in college was a Christian girl from the South. We argued often about whether the blacks were inferior and should be separated from the whites (her opinion). I spent a weekend with this friend and attended her large and beautiful church in Virginia. It just so happened that the Sunday I attended, a black family entered the church to worship, and were told to leave. I felt extremely uncomfortable and wondered whether if the church elders knew I was half-Chinese, I would be kicked out too. I scorned the various Biblical texts used to support the racial inferiority theories and injustice.

Later at Harvard I came to believe in Christ and realized that it wasn't the actions of so-called Christians that I should look to, but follow the example of Christ and His Word and the true Christians I encounter. I remembered a few godly professors at college, like our choir director Dean Arlton. He was a composer, music teacher, and role model, especially for our concert choir. Every Easter we traveled around in the NE U.S. and Canada for 2 weeks giving concerts of spirituals and classics. When we were asked to sing in 2 large prestigious churches and on the radio, but were to exclude our 2 black choir members (a bass and alto with beautiful solo voices for our spiritual pieces), as blacks were not allowed in the churches, Dean Arlton immediately refused. With these thoughts of holy men/women and the supreme role model of Christ, I came to a spiritual peace, though I still had many racial and cultural issues to grapple with.

When I went to Germany in 1968 to study medicine, I experienced a profound and bitter emotional upheaval. Looking back, I now recognize that what I went through was a deep culture shock. I had never heard the term "culture shock" then. This term, describing the phenomena of cross-cultural experiences, was coined by a Finnish/Canadian anthropologist in 1954 and wasn't in current usage yet. Since I had studied German language and culture in college, I went to Germany with knowledge, but idealizing its culture, its music, literature, art, as the height of European civilization. I soon found out that even though WW II ended 20 years before, there was still a deep vein of Nazism and racist thinking in Germans, especially among those 45 years of age or older. Some of our professors in medical school had a known Nazi past and were even on the "Brown list" (a list of active Nazi participants who committed crimes against humanity). They were prejudiced against foreign students and since many of our exams were oral, foreigners could easily be failed. One of the worst Nazi professors was an intelligent anatomist who gave lectures on Leonardo Da Vinci and Michelangelo's anatomical drawings; a cultured man, but one who hated foreigners. I had to suffer under his tutelage and was failed by him on one important exam that could have ended my days as a medical student if I didn't, on my repeat oral exam by him, have the support of the head of the Anatomical Institute and the Student Union President as witnesses.

When riding on the bus, the older Germans would often single out foreigners loudly and say: "there are too many foreigners, if Hitler was still alive, you wouldn't be here..." etc. Even educated people like my German friends' parents, after drinking a few beers, would start talking about how great the Nazi times under Hitler were. We foreigners were often unable to rent a room or get jobs, because there would be signs on the cards of the University bulletin board advertising for part-time jobs or rooms stating "no foreigners wanted". Sometimes on the phone I would say "I'm an American" and would go for the job interview or to see a room, and would be told, "but you're not American, you must have been born someplace else, Asia or South America." In the line-ups at the butcher's or deli or bakery I would often be ignored and/or pushed to the back of the line.

The Germans of the younger generation were not usually racist and were in fact rebelling against the ideas of their parents. But most of the German students turned to Socialism and Communism and were avidly anti-religious and anti-American, not just anti-Vietnam War. There were lots of sit-ins and protest actions. I felt as lost among them as I had felt in high school. So if I was discriminated against by the older generation of Germans for my olive skin and "exotic" looks, I was also criticized by fellow students for being a typical capitalist Christian American (disregarding the fact that our family existed below the poverty line). As my German language became more fluent, I would sometimes retaliate by asking the German students to look at the way their own country treated foreign students and "guest" workers.

It seemed like I could not tolerate remaining in Germany. I was not accepted for either of my heritages. I became very bitter and depressed. My disillusionment was profound. Were it not for the fellowship of the InterVarsity Christian group on campus, where there were German as well as foreign Christians from all over the world, I'm sure I would have become deranged. I spent many hours together with fellow Christians, talking, making music, studying the Bible and discussing all sorts of topics including literature and politics and how they relate to Christianity and to living a Christian life. We prayed together, went on retreats in the mountains, organized University lectures by Christian professors in Germany, attended concerts in the great churches in the city, worshipped together, and reached out to the alienated among the students.

It was during this time that I made friends with Asians: Chinese Indonesians, Koreans, Taiwanese, Japanese, and found that although we were from different countries, I had more in common with them in terms of humor and social interaction, than I had with many of the Europeans, the Germans, British etc. All these influences calmed me and when I finished my studies and internship, most of the bitterness and identity crisis I went through were abating. I also was beginning to see myself as a Chinese American, not one or the other.

My return to North America was a relief, and my Pediatric training was in Edmonton, Alberta, Canada. We had many fellow Interns and Residents who were overseas Chinese. We seemed to click instinctively and I became close with many Malaysian, Singaporean, and Hong Kong Chinese. Our sense of humor, the way we related to each other socially, and our interests were similar (except that I liked sports and mountain activities, and few of the other overseas Chinese did). I loved to cook and we shared our recipes. I could cook delicious soups, like shark's fins and bird's nest, and even crispy squab, as my father had taught me, and they in turn taught me how to make Hainan Chicken, Shanghai cold noodles, curries, etc.

In 1981, when China was just opening up to Western tourists, I arranged for my father, mother, cousin, and I to go on a group tour to China for 18 days. My father was thrilled to be returning to the land of his birth after 45 years in the U.S. Although we were not able to visit his poor home village in the Pearl River Delta, we did spend some days in Guangdong province. There, my father could speak his dialect (Toisan) and Cantonese to some extent. In the other places we visited, he would communicate with the Mandarin speaking locals by writing Chinese characters and receiving the written answers. He enjoyed himself thoroughly, and as for me, I was also amazed to be in Asia for the first time. I took hundreds of slides and photos. I went through a period of admiring everything Chinese, its history and culture. I read many books about Chinese history and the translated classics. I was proud of my Chinese heritage, but yet I knew my roots were not really in China, so I began to read literature by North American Chinese like Jade Snow Wong, Wayson Choi, Maxine Wong Kingston and felt a resonance, a realization "that's partly who I am, many of their experiences are my experiences too" (even though the authors were mainly of pure Chinese and not mixed racial origin).

I think my father, after so many years in the U.S., also felt alienated from his birthplace and culture, though he was happy to have had the opportunity to step foot on his land of birth again. It was on a Thanksgiving Day after that trip, that our family was all together in New York at the dinner table when my father indicated he wanted to speak. This was extremely unusual for him. In front of us all, including in-laws, he expressed his apologies for being such a stern, unaffectionate, and distant father. He said that the only way he knew to bring up children was from his own experience as an orphan, raised in a poor farming village, where conditions and discipline were harsh. He said that after living in the U.S. for so many years and observing the way Christian American parents raised their children, he felt there was a much better way to raise children than he had done. We were all in tears, knowing how difficult it was for him, (especially with his deeply ingrained Chinese cultural mindset of not losing face and not apologizing) to speak his regrets to us.

My reason for going into medicine was to help others and to serve. I wanted to be like the fine G.P. and Pediatrician who came to do house calls when we children, especially my brother David, who has Down's syndrome, were ill. I had long investigated the possibilities of being a missionary doctor, so I would have more opportunities to touch the body as well as the soul of those less fortunate than myself. I felt that although I had gone through many emotional and psychological trials, I had come through relatively intact. I was healthy and lived simply, and had been given the gift of intelligence and an education. The best way to thank God for these gifts was to pass this thankfulness on to others.

Dr. Albert Schweitzer influenced my thinking a lot. Initially I thought of South America, because I could speak Spanish, but I learned from other missionaries that I would have to take medical exams in Spanish before being permitted to work in most SA countries. I had just completed German, Canadian and American Exams, so I was not inclined to go through that stress again. I looked for other avenues of service after I finished my Pediatric training. I had the opportunity to go with a Christian relief organization to help out in the Vietnamese refugee camps of Malaysia for 6 months in 1982. I was first required to take an orientation course in Seattle with speakers from Seattle Pacific University, anthropologists, theologians etc. That was when I first learned the terms "cross-cultural", "culture shock", received an introduction to missiology, and learned how to live as a Christian in another culture. I enjoyed that course so much and it seemed to awaken me to the riches of a bicultural heritage.

Those 6 months in Malaysia, where I was Medical Officer in charge of a refugee camp in Sungei Besi with about 2000 refugees, many of them Chinese/Vietnamese, and where I did brief clinics on the receiving island of Pulau Bidong, I never felt any kind of culture shock. From the first morning I awoke to see the mists over mountains and palm trees, I was so entranced and happy, excited to be able to serve as I had always wanted. But I realize that things were made easy for me. First of all, we didn't live in the refugee camp itself. The Malaysian Government would not allow it. Our team lived on the outskirts of Kuala Lumpur in 2 large apartments. Our team consisted of young men and women volunteers, all Christian Americans, and 2 retired American Vietnamese missionaries. We got along well together. Everyday we were driven in the Red Crescent Society (Red Cross equivalent) or United Nations jeeps/trucks to the camp and back. We had pretty good Vietnamese/English interpreters, and the Malaysians who helped the personnel and us spoke good English.

In the evening we would seldom cook, but roam the streets and buy food from hawkers of many different nationalities. We ate curries on banana leaf, ngan, char kwei tiao, sate, laksa, chendol; we tried as many different foods as possible. Other than the heat, which I didn't tolerate well, I felt at home as I had never felt before. The church I attended (we were not allowed to attend the Vietnamese Sunday services in the camp except on special occasions) was a Presbyterian church with a mixed ethnic congregation, worshiping in English. I could hardly believe that they had 3 manual pipe organs, which the Malaysians had disassembled and hidden underground during World War II to prevent the Japanese from destroying it. I had taken 4 years of classical organ lessons and was overjoyed by the opportunity to be able to play for the Easter service, when the regular English organist was on vacation. (Where I lived in Canada there were few real pipe organs and no opportunities to play.) How could I not feel at home in a place where there were so many inexpensive delicious foods, lovely people of many ethnic backgrounds, and a good team to serve with. Culture shock was not a possibility!

In 1983, the opportunity came to serve as a Pediatrician in a mission hospital for mainly aboriginals in rural Taitung, Taiwan. When I received the invitation, I started learning Mandarin in earnest. Previously, I had already learned many characters over the years, but could not speak a word of Mandarin, only a bit of Cantonese, closer to my father's dialect. It was a small 50-bed hospital and I was to care for all the infants and children on the wards, in the OPD and Emergency room. I can truly say that I had very little time to learn more Mandarin or to absorb much Chinese culture. I lived with a lovely American nurse anesthetist, Carol Gunzel, who generously shared her apartment. This apartment was in a compound, which housed 3 apartments for single expatriate missionaries and an elementary school for missionary children. I spent most of my time in the hospital running from one emergency to the other, resuscitating newborns in the nursery, starting cut-downs on severely dehydrated and moribund infants, and doing exchange transfusions for intensely jaundiced neonates. Many of our little patients were referred from other hospitals as there were no other Pediatricians in the county, and the condition of the patients was serious. Since I often had to stay in the hospital all night, I was given a room across from the nursery, which I could use when I had critically ill patients. I can truly say sometimes I was working at least 120 hours/week.

A few of the national nurses spoke English, and I also had a national interpreter during the day who followed me around on my rounds, in OPD, in the Emerg. Dept. etc. The lack of language ability did cause me some frustrations, as well as the fact that the equipment and training of the young aboriginal nurses were not always what I was used to in Canada. On one hand, they were bright, lovely, and cooperative, and it seemed to me that I could help them improve, expand their skills, and increase their knowledge. I launched a series of classes on neonatal and pediatric topics and skills.

Although at times I struggled with relating to hospital authorities, I still wanted to return to Taitung, not just because of the medical and spiritual needs, but to encourage the aboriginal staff. It was a commitment out of this compassion for the underdog, wanting to stand together with them. Over the years God has enabled me to encourage some of them, and lift them from their feelings of inferiority. Some of these beloved co-workers have indeed gone on to obtain further education, university degrees and higher positions, and one even became a cross-cultural missionary.

I often felt torn between the circle of western missionaries versus that of the tribal nurses. I longed to get to know the local people with the little free time I had. I was disillusioned with the perhaps unconscious paternalism exhibited toward the nationals and overseas Chinese by some of the missionaries I otherwise admired and respected. I had some trouble adjusting to the worship style, religious language, and fundamentalist subculture as well. This presented a deeper adjustment to a Western subculture than to the local culture.

Fortunately God gave me the friendship of a wonderful, understanding overseas Chinese/American couple, Dr. Titus and Helen Loong and their daughters, who prayed with and for me, opened their home to me and advised me in many situations. Also, an older American medical couple, Dr. and Mrs. Tucker, were a great support to me, spiritually, emotionally and in medical questions. Dr. Tucker, a Harvard graduate, was born in China of 2 missionary doctors. Gradually, I was able to span 2 graduate worlds and make a few Taiwanese and Aboriginal friends. Titus and Helen gave me a plaque with a verse that was to be my inspiring verse as a missionary doctor: I will put my Spirit on my servant and he will bring justice to the nations – Isaiah 42:1.

After 7 months in Taiwan, I returned to Canada and practiced for a short time. Then I was off to Taipei to study Mandarin for 8 months at the Taiwan Normal University, looking towards future possibilities of further service in a Taitung. I disliked the large, crowded, polluted city of Taipei, which seemed to me to have no aesthetic qualities, and very few trees and greenery. The people of Taipei were unfriendly for the most part, not like the people of Taitung.

When in 1988 I was again asked to help out in Taitung, I was glad to do so. For the next 9 years, I spent about ½ of each year in Taiwan serving at the mission hospital, and ½ of each year in Canada, practicing medicine in Canada to support myself and my ministry in Taitung. During that time, since I was going back and forth, I didn't seem to have feelings of cultural displacement. My Mandarin improved and I had made many local friends. I would cringe whenever the expatriates would get together and complain about all sorts of things and issues that bothered them about Taiwanese or Aboriginal culture. I did not experience the emotional upheaval of several short-term missionaries who developed culture shock. I was less than humble; in fact I was secretly proud that I had never yet experienced true culture shock in Taiwan. Why should I, being half-Chinese and exposed to Chinese cultural influences from birth! I was to be proven wrong.

Beginning in 1998, I was given a stipend by the newly nationalized mission hospital in Taitung, and therefore I didn't need to spend half of each year practicing medicine in Canada to support my service in Taiwan. I never thought I would have problems adjusting culturally, just coping with the usual medical and professional difficulties and frustrations. I came closer to my Taiwanese and Aboriginal colleagues and deeper friendships developed. For the first time I felt the frustrations of feeling the differences in our cultural backgrounds. It was not the lawless driving, or the disregard for the rules or any of the other typical complaints of the expatriates that bothered me deeply. I discovered that the closer I got to a person in friendship, the more our cultural differences interfered and caused misunderstandings.

For example, I discovered that the Taiwanese and the Aboriginals (from which group I had the most friends) regarded friendship in an entirely different way. It was often hard to understand them and their social excuses. They would call at the last moment to break an appointment and just explain that "something had come up" ("Wo yo shih").

It seemed that they had a low commitment to friends but a high commitment to the large extended family that often overruled everything else, even if they were Christians. For example, if a 2nd or 3rd Uncle whom they had never seen or hadn't seen for 10 years, died, they would rush off to the funeral, a 4-5 hour or more drive away, or attend the wedding of the child of a 4th cousin whom they had met once, forgetting their promises/commitments to friends or to the church. The extended family being huge, this would often occur. An Aboriginal pastor's wife (former Pediatric Nursing Head at our hospital), who became a close friend, Helen Swun, once explained these difficulties to me in regards to church life.

Westerners including myself often admire the Chinese for their kinship and family commitments. Indeed it is sometimes touching to see how the young care for the older generation. But I have experienced the flip side of this sometimes rigid regard for family among my friends and colleagues that cause them great hardship. For example, often a whole family, most of them hardworking and trying to get ahead, and to get an education, would practically have to bankrupt themselves to pay off the gambling debts of a profligate and philanderer. I know a Pastor who cosigned a mortgage with his irresponsible and dishonest brother against the wishes of his wife. When the brother later refused to pay the mortgage, the Pastor was left with a huge debt, and had to sell his own house and move into an apantment. Meanwhile, the brother and his wife, who had both been working, bought a new house with their own money. It would pain and anger me to see my friends having to support other family members and their children's education, because the latter refused to get a job, or would drink his/her earnings away.

We all occasionally use social "lies" to prevent others from being hurt, or even to protect ourselves. The Taiwanese seemed masters and frequent users of this type of social evasion, which was often used to avoid causing others or themselves to lose face. But sometimes this type of dishonesty caused more harm...another point of difference that I tried to accept, and to understand the meaning "behind the spoken language".

The Taiwanese/Aboriginals seemed to become angry if they themselves were proven wrong. They would rarely apologize, even for an obvious mistake. I didn't understand this reaction until a Filipino/Chinese Surgeon pointed it out to me. It was difficult to reconcile under these conditions sometimes. An apology for an obvious wrong was never offered.

I enjoyed the warmth of the aboriginal personality, which was closer to my Spanish heritage, as opposed to the pragmatic, less emotional relationships with the Chinese Taiwanese. It seemed easy to become friends. However I sometimes experienced, (as Dr. George Lesley MacKay, the famous Canadian missionary to Northern Taiwan expressed in his autobiography "From Far Formosa", when describing the difference between Taiwanese and Aboriginals) that the emotions were short-lived and shallow.

Something I finally understood was a difference in entertaining friends. To us from the West, it is considered an honor to be invited to someone's home, to join the family, and eat food specially prepared by the hostess/host. But the Chinese must show respect by inviting their friends out to a restaurant, and usually in larger groups; the more noise the better. So, while I would love to invite a couple and their children, or a few friends to my apartment and cook for them, I felt that they didn't consider this as highly as if I asked them out to a restaurant. (Even though they liked the food I cooked and all the dishes were always clean!). They would have to have many guests, whereas I preferred to only have a few, so we could talk in depth and become closer, helping each other by sharing in a quiet environment.   Almost every time I invited friends, they would ask, "Who else is coming"? I would never ask such a question, which to my mind was impolite.

The closer I came to someone in friendship, the more I realized the gaps in our understanding of each other. In fact I could say, the closer the friendships, the more misunderstandings occurred. Sometimes I was deeply hurt; it is also probable that I hurt others, but the culture seemed not to allow for frank discussion of problems. However, I was able to discuss my hurts honestly with Helen Swun, and she helped in my appreciation of our differences and in accepting them.

I learned humility and forgiveness of self and others along my life's journey toward self-acceptance and self-understanding, and I have found a comfortable identity. As one grows older, one realizes that the identity crises that one goes through, the process of finding oneself, and accepting who one is and where one came from, though sometimes excruciatingly difficult, brings wisdom and compassion. Gradually, one realizes that whether one is of monoethnic background, or a bi- or tricultural, or multiracial origin, there are riches that God gives each one, in order that we may be distinct. I thank God for sending so many special friends my way, and mentors of different races and nationalities who have helped me along the difficult path of finding myself. Ultimately, the most important thing is to become what God created us to be, persons who will serve and help bring Christ's justice, love, and hope to others whom we encounter.

───

Dr. Florence On (1943 – 2007) served as a Pediatrician at Taitung Christian Hospital for two decades. She bonded deeply with the land and people; half of her ashes were buried in Taitung. Florence only began to reflect on her TCK identity a year before she was called to her eternal home. Though in great physical pain, her soul found peace and an anchor as she penned her story, slowly and painfully. In January 2007, with a brother's help, her long story was done to her satisfaction. Florence left us this gift which she could only imagine its significance.

Camp Reflection

Karen Wong

In July 2007, Sky and Karen planned and ran a camp for MKs in Hong Kong. Below is Karen's summary of the camp, which includes reflections on her own life as a MK. Mission agencies and churches can consider sponsoring MKs to return to their parents' home country during the summers for camps, career internships, to teach English, or to study Chinese. The idea is to let them make like-minded friends, learn useful skills and their parents' first language, and be acquainted with the culture and society in creative ways. More and more MKs will choose to return to their parents' home country for university education. It is not too much to suggest that churches can sponsor these youths to fly back to their parents' home country during the summer if they wish to. - Editor -

It all started with Sky Siu, Cindy Loong, and I. We all came together during a lunch meeting and began to talk of the idea of having a MK camp. However, our busy schedules stopped us from continuing to plan, until I realized that Hong Kong Alliance Mission would be having an anniversary with a large group of missionary families returning to Hong Kong that summer. Then, I realized that this would be an opportunity to get the kids together and to run the camp. The camp was initially prepared for 5 to 6 kids, and it was meant to be a small camp rather than a big one.

Around March, the planning became more intense and detailed. Around the month of May, we started to look for a campsite. Auntie Helen (Cindy's mother) kindly volunteered to search for a campsite and find financial support. Finally, we decided on High Rock in Shatin to be the campsite.

However, due to our busy schedules, and Cindy being away in the States, we didn't have time to visit the campsite until a week before the camp.

We began to send letters out to missionaries around the month of June, and gradually attendees gathered and signed up for the camp. I was quite amazed. There were several I knew from Dalat International School in Malaysia, and also from my parents' mission field. The schedule was set, and looking back, I am still amazed how we managed to plan everything in spite of all the chaos that was going on in all our leaders' lives.

On the first day, we met up with Gordon, MK ministry staff of Hong Kong Association of Christian Missions, for lunch, to talk about the camp, and to run through some final logistics. Then, the kids came, and we met up at the Shatin KCR (train station).

We went up to High Rock Camp together and settled down. We started out with some ice breaker games and got to know each other. The camp was planned for 15 - 18 year old youths. Many of them were not shy and they were very active and cooperative with the games that Sky and I had prepared for them. I also noticed how several of them began to talk to one another, and the girls warmed up with each other faster.

One of the games that we played was "I have" instead of the usual "I have never," in a fruit basket style. This game helped each kid to talk about the unique things they had done. Those who had never done the thing that the person in the center mentioned would have to change seats. Kids began to find similarities with fellow campers, and also come to understand that they were indeed special. The game was followed by a simple sharing by Cindy, Sky and I. The youths in general were very attentive.

On the second or third morning, Sky and I got together and prayed before we had our fellowship. I really felt God's Spirit moving as we prayed.

I was amazed at how well-behaved the campers were, and how willing they were to join in the activities that Sky and I had prepared. Not only that, but we also caught them conducting devotions on their own in the mornings with no instructions given by us.

By watching them, I was challenged and encouraged at the same time. I grew up in Dalat, a Christian international school in Malaysia. Since graduating from high school, I have talked with several of my friends from Dalat, and heard stories about my peers. Some have adjusted well in their new environment, while some have turned away from God. I believe every missionary kid is susceptible to such a danger.

Kids are often the victims, but also the benefactors of their parents' work. They get the firsthand experience of God's work, but sometimes it comes with a great price. During our time at the camp, we were able to address some of the issues that we encountered as missionary kids. Some kids mentioned not being able to spend time with parents and being left at home alone from time to time. Some kids were sent to boarding school at a very young age, thus creating a relational gap with their parents. But despite their experiences and pain, they all showed great care for their parents' ministry in one way or another, and it was something precious that it really touched me.

It was weird running the camp, as I was seeing things from the "other side". But interestingly enough, I saw a lot of myself in the kids. Despite their playfulness and silliness, each and every one of them showed a sense of maturity when it came to understanding their parents' ministry and what it takes. If you were to ask the kids, they could easily give you an explanation of their parents' ministry, and what their parents are trying to achieve in the mission field.

The camp provided a place for the kids to feel free to openly share their frustrations. It is hard for kids when they are with their parents on the mission field; a lot of them were even required to be co-workers with their parents. However, by being surrounded by other missionary kids at this camp, they did not need to guard themselves; they also didn't have to explain to others regarding their identity as a "MK". They could simply be themselves. I may have over analyzed some of the situations, but many of the things I've shared also apply to me. Often times, I feel encouraged and relaxed when I'm hanging out with other MKs, because it is a safe place where you don't have to do much explaining for others to understand you. Each of the participants have experienced their share of pain in cultural adjustment, language barrier, separation from parents, and ultimately, the simple obedience.

As I always share in different churches, I never wanted to become a missionary at the age of 6 when my parents decided to pack up their bags and move to Japan. I didn't feel God's calling at the age of 14 when they believed it was their time to move to Thailand and to obey what God had planned for them. It wasn't my decision to want to be enrolled in a boarding school. However, all those "it wasn't my decision" comprise and structure who I am today. I believe all those "it wasn't my decision" were one of the common things that we all shared in the camp. Despite how many things we as missionary kids have experienced that have been contrary to our desires, each and every one of us have learned to embrace our lives one way or the other. The wonderful thing about the camp was that I truly believed that the youths wanted to be there and that it was a great experience for each and every one of them.

I have shared in one of my sharing times that as a teenager, before I came back to Hong Kong to study, I didn't remember Hong Kong being a fun place. To me, Hong Kong was a drag and I detested it. The idea of routine church visits, questions about things that seemed trivial to me, and the constant critiques by others about my Cantonese or the way I held my chopsticks, were not things I looked forward to.

The camp allowed us to become friends, especially those who were returning to Hong Kong, either alone or with their parents. It was actually a way to change their views about Hong Kong. Even after the camp, I know that several of them took the initiative to hang out. Ultimately, that was the goal I believe God wanted us to achieve. Instead of getting the kids to understand themselves more as missionary kids (although that is important), more importantly, we created a place where kids from similar backgrounds were able to find another person to just share their lives with. It was about "living together".

Some of the kids who participated in the camp didn't go to boarding school, and some did. Despite differences, everyone was able to just hang out and talk. However, coming out of the camp, I felt a greater burden for the kids, because I saw so much of myself in each of them. I cannot say my missionary kid life was a wonderful one; there were many ups and downs. It is really by God's mercy that I am able to reflect today and be grateful about it. One of my prayers now is to pray that each and every one of the missionary kids will come to see the gift that God has given them. I pray that instead of turning their backs on their identity and experiences, they will be able to accept the healing that God can provide through His grace and love.

Karen Wong and her sister Joyce grew up in Hong Kong, Japan, Thailand, and Dalat International school of Malaysia. Karen is completing her studies at Hong Kong University.

What Does a Godly Life Look like?

Jane Lo

I have learned that the beauty of the Christian life lies not in the hope of perfection attained on earth, but in the assurance that despite one's many imperfections, God's grace remains. And this is the life that I, too, desire.

I once believed that a godly life was probably marked by a lot of "Christian good works": Bible studies, memory verses, Sunday School attendance, good marks in Bible class, tithing in church, and praying aloud from time to time when called upon. By these markers, my life was in pretty good shape. I have learned since then that without Christ, it would never be enough to do all these, or even more. No number of Sunday school attendance stickers would ever be enough to cover my sin. Not even a lifetime of sermons preached or Bible studies led can pave the path to Christ. It is by His grace alone – a truth that rings true even for a pastor, his wife, and his children.

I was born into a family where God and His church were and continue to be a top priority. Many of my earliest childhood memories are of church events: a musical performance at Christmas time where I played the role of a wrapped gift, a particularly memorable Sunday service that suddenly had to be held outdoors in a nearby park, for a reason I can no longer remember, home group meetings that were always noisy, and potlucks as well. Specific Sunday school lessons and sermons do not come to mind when I think back to the days in Vancouver when my parents pastored the Lord's Love Church, but they must have stayed with me, for it was never difficult to recall the story of Moses, or Joshua, or David. Their successes, their failures before

God – these have been ingrained into my young mind long before I could remember.

Returning to Hong Kong from Vancouver was nothing like the traumatic experience it could have been for a six-year-old. Looking back on those first few months, only good memories come to mind. I remember my parents' obvious pleasure as they looked out the apartment window that first night and saw, instead of the pitch darkness of a Vancouver neighborhood, the rows and rows of lights in the buildings across from our own, each lit window representing a family still awake and about. I still recall how amazed I was with the mall decorations in front of our new apartment complex the first time I saw them. I had never seen Christmas lights so generously hung on such tiny trees. "It's so beautiful!" I kept thinking to myself. "Hong Kong is so beautiful."

I proceeded to start the first of my eleven years in the International Christian School, a place where Bible classes were strictly required for every one of those eleven years, and where learning about God from teachers who loved Him was a part of the daily schedule. Singing worship songs in chapel, listening to Bible stories and their real-life applications, doing sword drills and memorizing scripture – these activities, so decidedly Christian, became second nature to me. I learned the code of conduct expected of "good" Christians and followed it carefully, never swearing, never listening to the "wrong" kinds of music or watching the "wrong" kinds of movies, and never copying homework.

It was not until years later that I learned that there was more to the Christian walk than simply staying on the right side of the line, the line people could see. There was more to calling oneself a follower of Christ than keeping a haughty eye out for naughty classmates who did all those forbidden activities. "I am so good," I would think to myself. "I never swear." I was careful to keep my outward actions pleasing, but looking back on my middle school years; I was also one of the nastiest thirteen-year-olds ever. I was the mastermind behind a chain of prank emails that were sent to a very lonely and unpopular girl in my grade. I pretended to be a secret admirer of hers, and found it terribly funny to read her replies and share them with my friends. In front of her, of course, I was the friendliest and kindest of souls.

I look back on the incident today and understand that there is little I can ever do to erase the damage that was done. Several years passed before my conscience finally urged me to seek forgiveness from her, when I finally found the courage to e-mail her. Her reply was troubling yet not terribly surprising – those years had been so unbearable for her that she had sought counseling. Hers was not the first apology I wrote. My conscience seemed to come to life for the first time that summer, the sent folder in my email account overflowing with typed apologies to everyone from an older brother to a sixth grade teacher. I remember revealing, for the first time, the way I had taken money from my parents' drawer, or the way I had lied about a broken camera. "I gossiped about you that year," I would say to a friend. "I'm so sorry and really wish you would consider forgiving me." "I wrote that note. I wish I could take back what I said because I know it hurt you."

The reality of my sin-laden life had never seemed so real. The fact that I had been born and raised in a Christian home, and was the child of a respected pastor, did not mean immunity from sin or its consequences. The blessed truth of my faith in Jesus Christ is that my sin has already been covered by the blood that He shed for me on the cross. He knew that no amount of Bible verses memorized or Bible tests aced could ever save my dirty soul, so he paid the price in full, long in advance.

I have grown up watching my parents lead lives that are pleasing to the Lord in many ways. My father is a man of God who has devoted his life to furthering the Kingdom through his preaching, leadership in missions, and gospel radio organizations. My mother is a godly woman who has been reaching many needy lives as a social worker, Bible study leader, and Sunday school teacher. Yet, even a pastor and his God-fearing wife have faults. As their child, I have seen firsthand what wonderful work they have done for God, but I have also seen the mistakes they have made and the ways that they, too, have grieved the Spirit.

The apostle Paul writes in II Corinthians 12:10 "That is why, for Christ's sake, I delight in weaknesses...for when I am weak, then I am strong." As the child of a pastor, verses like this were often quoted and often memorized, but it was not until after the summer of 2006 that I truly understood what Paul's words meant. I joined a group of Christians on a missions trip to the province Hubei, where we led a week-long English camp for middle school students. Phonics, grammar, and vocabulary were taught, but the real reason for our presence in that small city of Huangshi was that we might lead these children to Christ through our love for them. The week was a difficult one for me, for although the trip was a mere nine days in duration, I felt exceedingly homesick and also very discouraged because I felt greatly intimidated by our task of evangelism.

One afternoon, when the students were working in groups, another camp leader and I began chatting about the week's events in the back of the classroom, and he told me the wonderful news that each of the twelve students in his group had already heard the gospel once, and several had gone on to commit their lives to the Lord. As I told him that I had only shared the gospel with one student, and saw that she had not expressed interest in the faith, quick tears came to my eyes and I began to cry. I so wished that they would come to know my Jesus, and still they had not yet heard His message of love to them. The students in my group noticed my tears and quickly came to my side. "Why is she crying?" they kept asking the camp leader I had been speaking with. "It is because she loves you," he told them. It was in my moment of greatest weakness that the students were most interested in what I had to tell them, and I was able to share the gospel with them that afternoon. Two girls in my group accepted Jesus right then, and by the end of the week a total of seven students in my group had come to know the Lord. God showed me that it is in my weakness that he becomes my strength and that in my imperfections, my only hope.

I am a Christian today, a twenty-year-old with dreams of mirroring my parents' lives of ministry. I do not know whether Jesus will mold me into a missionary, a social worker, or a parent who raises her children in the ways of the Lord, but I know that I am willing and eager to follow whatever path He has directed for me. I admire my parents for being people who use the gifts God has blessed them with. The Bible studies led, the sermons preached, and the seminars given are not a means of buying salvation, but of responding in love to the price it cost. As their child, I have learned that the beauty of the Christian life lies not in the hope of perfection attained on earth, but in the assurance that despite one's many imperfections, God's grace remains. And this is the life that I, too, desire.

Jane Lo is currently a student at the University of British Columbia in Vancouver and pursuing a double major in English Literature and Religious Studies. She is passionate about God, music, her family, and her friends.

God Is In Control

Titus Yu

One most important principle is that wherever you go, you have to respect and appreciate the cultural differences of the local people, and be prepared to be flexible in terms of accepting the differences. The more you respect and appreciate the easier and faster you can integrate into the local community and your local colleagues.... God always has a special purpose for putting one in a particular position, for example in business leadership. My mother and wife always remind me to be a humble servant in high positions.

I was born in Singapore during the time when my parents studied Theology at the Discipleship Training Centre. Just a few weeks after my birth, my parents brought me back to Hong Kong. I was born with a heart problem, and had to undergo several treatments and was required to take medication constantly during my childhood. By God's grace, I gradually recovered from my heart problem when I became a teenager. I was brought up in Hong Kong, where my father was a pastor, and later served in Hong Kong Churches' Renewal Movement. My mother was a secondary school teacher. I grew up attending church due to direct influence and discipline from my parents. I knew all the Bible stories in my head, but Jesus Christ was not in my heart and had not become my personal savior.

During my teenage period, attention and energy were focused on sports, computer games and schoolwork. I did not remember attributing to God for my good grades at school, but instead claimed them as my personal achievements. I was too proud of myself. At university, I spent all my energy on hostel activities, still not paying attention to my spiritual life. Non-Christian peers surrounded me and I did not take Jesus Christ seriously as my Lord. I gradually stopped attending church.

After many years of earnest prayers and much admonition by my parents, I was finally willing to attend the youth fellowship in a church. In the fellowship, I met Christian peers and began to appreciate their commitment to Christ. I started reflecting upon myself in regards to my relationship with Jesus.

One turning point was in the late 90's when I was struck by an acute viral attack in my inner left ear when I was working in Singapore. My ear became swollen, and suddenly, I could not hear anything with my right ear. The doctor in Singapore was not able to treat me, so I had to immediately fly back to Hong Kong, and was admitted to the hospital for another treatment. During the week in hospital, I reflected again upon my relationship with Jesus, and repented for having gone astray from Him. I realized that Jesus has total control of my life, and that God's will is sovereign over everything that happens to me, including this acute viral attack. After a week of special treatment, by God's grace, I was able to recover 70% of the hearing ability of my left ear. I am convinced that this was not a coincidence, and that God really wanted to let me know that He has total control of my life.

Being an Expatriate for Christ

I really thank God for giving me the opportunity to work in different countries and in cross-cultural settings. Over the last 10 years, I have worked in different countries including Hong Kong, China, Singapore, Guam (USA) and Bangkok. Here are some of my experiences that I can share with others in regards to working/living in cross-cultural settings. The toughest challenge is usually the first 3 to 6 months of working/living in a foreign country. One has to adjust to almost everything within a very short period of time including the climate, culture, people, food, accommodations, commuting, etc.

In the workplace it is especially difficult because you do not know your new colleagues in depth, yet the company already starts to demand performance from you/your team. Within a very short period of time you have to know the colleagues around you, the organizational structure, the culture of the company, the work ethics of that country, taboos to be avoided, people you can trust or not trust, office politics, hidden business crisis, etc. in order for you to start 'phasing-in' to your new job. All these, when added up, are quite stressful to a person. Apart from work, one also has to adjust to family, church, and social life.

However, one most important principle is that wherever you go, you have to respect and appreciate the cultural differences of the local people, and be prepared to be flexible in terms of accepting the differences. The more you respect and appreciate, the easier and faster you can integrate into the local community and your local colleagues, which is a prerequisite of performing well in your new job as an expatriate.

As a Christian, before anything, it is critical to find a church where one can get spiritual and social support. My wife and I are glad that God has prepared churches for us wherever we have gone; big and small, with wonderful pastors and brothers & sisters from different countries who have become our angels, helping us to settle down in the new environment. We have spent most of our weekends with all the loving brothers & sisters from cell groups, participating in Bible studies, gatherings, sports, dinners, etc. and God has given us a lot of wonderful memories. We continue to keep in touch with them even though we left the country after only 12 to 18 months.

God also let us see the situation and various needs of His churches in different countries. We have had a chance to serve Him in various church settings, from big sized Baptist churches in Singapore and Bangkok with hundreds of members, to a very small Chinese congregation in Guam with only a few families, and where the Sunday service is conducted in a room of 25 square meters rented from a Korean church. When you are in a foreign country, God often will open the door for you to serve Him in unthinkable ways. My Mandarin is quite poor since I seldom practiced it when I was in Hong Kong. However, God used my very poor Mandarin to teach Sunday school to the youth and lead an adult Bible study in Bangkok and Guam, respectively. I could never have imagined that God would use me in such ways. God amazes me, that He has His own way of using His people to build up His church, as long as one is willing to commit himself/herself.

Wherever I went, I saw people living in various classes and conditions; I learned to respect both the rich and the poor, knowing that God loves them all. As an expatriate businessman, I count it my privilege to help the needy in the local community, and be grateful for what God has provided for me today.

A missionary friend of mine once told me that God always has a special purpose for putting one in a particular position, for example in business leadership. My mother and wife always remind me to be a humble servant in high positions, because I used to be too proud of myself. One senior executive of my company once said in a speech that he has 4 priorities before his career/company which are "his wife and three daughters". Someone said, "fall in love with your job but not with your company". I am still learning about all these, but believe these are some valuable guiding principles for people who have a similar background as I.

Titus was married to Vienne in 2002. After working in the Southern Pacific islands, and then in Bangkok for several years, Titus' career has taken him to East Asia. They have a one-year-old daughter Dorcas. In 21st century terminology, Titus and Vienne live their lives as cross-cultural tentmakers.

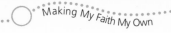

The Blessings of Being a Pastor's Kid

Julia Hu Chan

Like many missionaries, my parents were away during most weekends and school holidays because of pastoral or mission work. I was a girl who did not like to join in any games, because deep down inside, I feared losing. On the other hand, I was always seeking attention and wanting to feel important. How have I become the person I am today? I have to give credit to my parents.

As I reflect upon my life as a missionary and pastor's kid, I think the best thing about being one is the "ease" of looking for the will of God. I trust my parents, and they trust God, so when I listen to them, I'm listening to God. But of course, my "realization" did not come without much struggle between what I want for myself and what God wants for me...

I was born in Hong Kong while my parents were missionaries there, teaching in the Alliance Bible Seminary. I spent my wonderful childhood on one of Hong Kong's offshore islands called Chueng Chau. The whole family moved back to Singapore, where I finished high school. I later moved on to graduate with a biology degree in the United States. That summer, I went alone on a missions trip to Hong Kong. It turned out to be "longer-term missions"!

I have become a teacher in a local special school in Hong Kong for physically and intellectually challenged children for the past 16 years. I remember two students died during my first year of teaching. I felt very sad not only because of the loss, but because I had not shared Jesus with them. I wept and prayed that God would give me the strength and opportunity to share with every student that I come across, because I was sure that was why He sent me there.

My parents supported me and called me a "Missionary Teacher" since I was reaching a special community that is "unreached" by the local church. In the process, I have led many students to Jesus and continue to teach them with the Word of God. More than 20 students went home to be with the Lord, and I thank God that I did not let Him down, but have become His messenger in time.

Many may compliment that I must be a very loving and caring person to be doing such a job. However, when I was young, I was very insecure. Like many missionaries, my parents were away during most weekends and school holidays because of pastoral or mission work. I was a girl who did not like to join in any games, because deep down inside, I feared losing. On the other hand, I was always seeking attention and wanting to feel important.

How have I become the person I am today? I have to give credit to my parents. What did my parents do? They invited my brother and I to be little helpers while they were serving different people during the week. Apart from Bible teaching during the daytime, they were also involved in some local community ministries. I remembered we would sing at a local orphanage every week, and once in a while, also conduct activities with mentally challenged children. The most wonderful memories were of every Christmas, when our house would be packed with children, while I helped prepare food and set the table for all our dinner guests. The joy and satisfaction on their happy faces were unforgettable! Without realizing, the seed of empathy and love for less fortunate children had already been planted deep within my heart.

The Challenges of being a Missionary / Pastor's Kid

On the other side of the coin, MKs and PKs are very vulnerable under the spotlight of their parents' great ministry. What I mean is that when people see how godly and wonderful our parents are, they project similar expectations on us, too. Spoken or not, we were somehow expected to be present at every church event. People give us that strange look when we miss a verse or give wrong answers to Bible quizzes. If you are learning the piano, you should be able to play during children's worship. When it comes to electing the president of the youth fellowship, guess who gets the most votes?

However, our wrongdoings are also magnified somehow. My peers used to tease me "Oh look! See who's falling asleep during her dad's sermon!" "How can you date a non-Christian? You're the Pastor's daughter!" When I was young, I used to think that was so unfair!

When I was studying in the US, I had a very close friend, also a missionary kid, who became very depressed, and even attempted suicide. There was another MK, who was under so much pressure that he gave up on church altogether. The spiritual battle is on, between Satan and the servants of the Lord. The enemy is constantly looking for footholds to attack those who claim to love God. My observation and conclusion is that if they cannot find any "flaws" in the big guys, they go after the little ones – that's us. I bet their favorites are the rebellious teenagers. I can't imagine what would have happened to my parents' ministries if I had married a non-Christian or committed suicide. (Frankly, these thoughts had indeed crossed my mind during my teenage years, but I thank God for His protection. I know my parents prayed hard for me during those years!) Sadly, the fact is, many missionaries have left their ministries due to "children related matters".

Today, I am blessed to be a pastor's wife. Now I have two pastor's kids myself, and I realize the gravity of overlooking the importance of teaching my children according to God's way. I have sat through our church's children's Bible quizzes, where my children have missed obviously easy questions. I have seen how my own children would laugh at a fat boy at church. It is truly embarrassing! But instead of blaming my kids and adding pressure on them, I take it as a warning sign that I might be overlooking the fact that they are also in a spiritual battle. If they are not aware of how vulnerable they are, and are not growing in the Word of God, they will easily become targets of our enemy. Now I know why my parents insisted reading a verse before each dinner, why we had Tuesday night family worship times, bedtime stories, and spent time praying for everyone each night when we were young. I really appreciate the effort my parents put into preparing us for the "battle".

My husband and I are trying our best to follow our parents' footsteps, not for the sake of carrying on tradition, but because we realize it is our responsibility to equip our children, who are also living under the spotlight.

Julia grew up in a pastor's family that lived and served in Hong Kong and Singapore. She and her husband, Dickson, also a pastor, are currently serving in HK. Julia is a teacher of special education. They have one daughter, Joyce, and one son, Joseph.

From Loss to Gain

Samuel Lee

"What my parents did right was that when facing the drastic differences between the two generations, they cared more about the intentions and the spiritual meanings rather than appearance; they accepted those differences as long as they weren't against the truth nor arousing lust and temptations, which not only enabled me to develop my own style, i.e. baggie T shirts and jeans, but at the same time gave me a clear bottom line of God's truth."

"For whoever wants to save his life will lose it, but whoever loses his life for Me and for the Gospel will save it." Reading this scripture takes me only twenty seconds, but fully experiencing the meaning of it has taken me twenty years. Apparently, I own many things that others envy, such as my first music album, outstanding schoolwork, and an active social life. This makes some people think: "Well, Samuel can have such enviable achievements because he has clear dreams and goals, and he works hard at them."

However, when looking back at my twenty-two years of life, I cannot but admit: God has given me all of these. In the following sections, I would like to share three major turning points in my life, all during which I lost something seemingly precious, but gained eternal and godly treasures, which are far more valuable than all those worldly pleasures.

Before unfolding my past, I would first like to briefly introduce my family background in which I grew up. My father is the National Director of Taiwan Campus Crusade for Christ, and he and my mother are both speakers and marriage counselors. Instead of forcefully dragging me to church and Sunday school, my parents left me much space to make my own decision for Christ. When I was in third grade, one day, my father shared the gospel with me using the Four Spiritual Laws, and I received Christ as my Savior. That day marked the beginning of my personal relationship with God, which eventually deeply influenced my days to come.

Losing the Approval of Friends, but Gaining the Character of Humility

In sixth grade, there came a homeroom teacher who was a perfectionist, resulting in countless conflicts between her and our whole class. For example, after school, she usually wouldn't let us go home until we were in perfect order, but we considered her too faultfinding. When we criticized her of neglecting students' opinions, she thought of us as too childish and selfish. As the days went by, the misunderstanding between her and us went from bad to worse, which finally led to this unforgettable event.

One afternoon, during the Natural Science class, my classmates could not help but pour out all their anger and discontentment, listing the homeroom teacher's faults, one by one, to our subject teacher, who was kind-hearted and loving, and who patiently listened to our complaints. Talkative as I was, the opportunity of becoming the spokesperson of the class was too good to miss. Therefore, after raising my hand, I was permitted to speak, and I stood up to uncover more unreasonable deeds of our homeroom teacher.

However, as I was talking away, a hushed scream slipped out from my fellow classmates' mouths, forecasting something really bad was happening—our homeroom teacher had walked into the back door of the classroom. The subject teacher quickly bid me to sit down and immediately turned to the blackboard to continue the class, but everyone knew it was too late. Just as the bell rang, a loud growl was heard from the back of the room: "Samuel, You COME HERE!" accompanied by her noisily setting the chair down, and the gloomy expressions of my friends. I could hear the ominous prelude of the tempest of my life. Regarding what happened next, I only had a blurry impression - her seemingly endless rebukes flew by my ears like rains of arrows, and I lowered my head, gazing at the ground, twisting my fingers in my back, wishing I could just survive the ordeal.

The class bell rang, and I was freed. As I returned to my seat, some classmates passed me slips of papers to assure me of their support. But, suddenly a voice sprang out from my heart, which I believed must have been the voice of God, whispering to me: "This is not going to end here. Samuel, you HAVE TO apologize to your homeroom teacher, whom you had offended, as soon as possible." So, for the rest of science class, I was waiting for the crucial moment to come—the moment that I had to humble myself and say sorry to the one I respected least.

Again, the bell rang and I was about to carry out God's command. However, my friends tried their best to prevent me from such a stupid action: "She is not worthy of your apology," "…if you say sorry to her, I'll quit being friends with you!" Facing their threats and disapproval, the voice inside me still urged me to step out onto this narrow path. So there, standing before the teacher, with all my strength, I apologized to her word by word: "Teacher, I am sorry. Would you forgive me?" Upon receiving my apology, she continued her unfinished scolding in return. Even worse, when I returned to my seat again, I had to face the mockery from my fellow classmates: "Boy, are you a coward! Don't you have any guts in you?" I thought I had chosen the right path, but I did not win my teacher's forgiveness, let alone my friends' support.

Under such enormous frustration, amazingly, a peaceful feeling gradually ascended from my heart, blocking my mind from the surrounding criticism. I had seemingly done the most stupid thing in my life, but deep down in my heart, I knew this was the right thing to do. After school, as the students prepared to go home, I was called into the teachers' office to see my science subject teacher, who wanted to have a talk with me. I was ready for another scolding within the same day, but I only felt her gently patting my shoulder, speaking softly: "Samuel, I saw you say sorry to your homeroom teacher. I have to say, that was a mature act surpassing your age. I guess even some adults are still learning that lesson."

On that day, I did not receive forgiveness from my homeroom teacher, and I seemingly lost precious approval from friends momentarily, but it was also on that day I found out that humbling oneself and saying sorry isn't the hardest thing to do.

Losing the Chance for Romance, but Winning Pure Friendship

Leaving my childhood, I went into puberty, facing numerous changes within me, physically and mentally. All of a sudden, I became conscious of the existence of another species - females - sharing the same world with me. It was the first time that I realized whenever girls appeared, my eyes would go out of control, and every word they spoke and every step they took could strike the strings of my heart.

When I was in high school, I had a crush on a girl.

Did I know her?
 …I only knew her name…
Did I know her WELL?
Um…honestly…not really…
…but that was not important, for her beautiful face had already made me head over heels. For the very first time, I took a glance at the wondrous

chemical effects of this thing called "love." Ever since then, around dinner table, the subject of our family conversation switched from dinosaurs, robots, and ET, all the way to whatever related to that girl.

Based on their professional counseling experiences, my parents patiently listened to my daily tabloid anecdotes, even though they knew very well that what I had was a crush, and merely an illusion. As they observed, however, this "crush" had gradually become an obsession, and my mind had become unconsciously occupied by it. As a result, mother made use of this opportunity to teach me a lesson: Mutual attraction between the opposite sexes is normal, but that does not mean one should be overpowered by that seemingly common desire. God created us as sexual beings, but our sexual drives can be easily distorted into sinful lust. Scripture praises the sacredness and the pleasure of love, but at the same time, it teaches us to "guard our heart above all else."

One ordinary day, as usual, I walked by the girl and tried hard to find a subject to open up a conversation: "Hi, nice weather, isn't it? How is your recent practice for the guitar performance?"

The girl smiled and said: "Pretty good. You've got to come and see my performance, won't you?"

"N...no...no problem..."

The girl continued: "Oh by the way, don't forget to present me with flowers on stage."

"Flo...flowers!?"

This would be the biggest day of my life: The girl I liked asked me to bring her flowers, and give them to her on stage!? Faced with such a crucial decision, I knew I must consult with the two professional consultants in my home.

On hearing this latest news, my mother replied first: "Flowers? Giving the girl flowers? Then what next? Ask her to become your girlfriend? Then I guess you will want to hold her hands. And then what? What do you expect to come next in this physical contact process? You're only high school students; the relationship will go nowhere! ......" I believed mother's answer was "No!"

Smiling at me as usual, father gave me a camera and offered me an alternative: "Take this. Just take a picture. It is better than the fading flowers."

So there I was, at the concert hall. Within my hand was the steel, cold, lifeless camera, not the passionate red roses. As the performance began, the girl started playing the guitar and my mind as well. It was Canon in D by Pachelbel. As more and more players joining into the chord progression, the tension within me rose as well. "Should I, or should I not? Should I, or should I not?" The music stopped and the performance was over, and the girl, with thirty other performers, stood up to receive the roaring applause from the audience, which completely drowned out my last hopes to impress her.

Suddenly, the front line of the audience stirred. About six boys left their seats, ran to the edge of the stage, and piled their bodies on top of each other, making a human staircase. Just when everyone was in the midst of astonishment, another boy strode out from his seat, with a huge bouquet of flowers in hands, and then, stepping on his friends' backs, proudly headed toward the girl, the throne of his victory. The audience went wild, shouting, screaming and whistling: "That was AWESOME!!" But I also heard a different commentary: "Samuel, YOU LOST!!" Indeed, that evening, I did not get anyone's attention, and even worse, it seemed that the girl's heart was stolen by that boy with his bold attempt!

Yet, amazingly, the friendship between the girl and I was kept unspoiled, all because I had chosen to obey my parents, who were the authority that God had set over my life. Not only until that day did I begin to learn to build pure friendships with the opposite sex, looking into their inner qualities and characteristics, regardless of how they look on the outside. Then, one day, I made this prayer to God:

"Lord, I know that I'm not mature enough to fall in love, but my heart is still filled with fondness and admiration for her. You know me best, so please cool down this passion by all means, for I know that falling in love at such an age is not Your will." It was not easy for me to say this prayer, but it became the key moment in surrendering my desires to God.

Eventually, the girl had a boyfriend, and I could often see them interact intimately on campus. My friends felt sorry for me. However, anyone who knew my secret prayer would give thanks to God, for He did grant my prayer. I missed the chance to fall in love with the girl, but I experienced the purity of true friendship. I didn't win the girl's heart; therefore I could love God with all my heart and all my strength.

Abandoning My Ambition, Regaining God's Vision

I moved on to enter college life, an unfamiliar world, where the enormous pressure of the college entrance exam and the supervision from our parents, which we had long endured, suddenly disappeared. This sudden freedom would result in college freshmen's indulgent lifestyles, in which skipping class and immoral sexual relationships were common phenomena on campus. Living within this fallen world, I prayed to God:

"Make me a beacon in this spiritual wasteland!" When the semester began, I made the promise to God: "I want to live a godly life; my relationship with God will always be my top priority, study will be second, social life third, then my hobby—street dance will come last. Lord, I am ready to become light and salt to this darkened campus!!"

Perhaps because of my parents, I first attended the Campus Crusade for Christ Fellowship (CCC Fellowship); then, driven by my hobby, I also signed up for the Street Dance Club. As days passed, I put more and more effort into dancing, and spent more and more time on my schoolwork as well as other extracurricular activities. Sometimes, alone in my dorm room, I saw my Bible laying under the computer keyboard, and I knew that I'd been far from God, but I argued back with my conscience: "Hey! There are occasions, such as the summer mission trips, where my talents in choreography will be needed to serve God. Besides, I can share the Gospel with my friends in the Street Dance Club." At that moment, God did not argue back. I left the room and shut the door, leaving my Bible untouched, covered by the pile of things which I considered much more important than God's Word.

Half the semester had passed, and my life was completely out of control. My top priority, which should have been God, was replaced by dancing. Following this wrong priority, my schoolwork and social life were in a mess. Whenever the class bell rang, its loud and clear ring was like a slave driver, hurrying me to catch up with the chaotic schedule. Every day, when I went back to my room after dance practice, it was deep into the night. When I was ready to do my schoolwork, it was already two o'clock in the morning. As a result, trying to have more time to sleep one morning, I thought of skipping class for the very first time, when I suddenly realized: I was no different from non-Christians. The light of life within me that once had wanted to light up the fallen world had been swallowed up, bit-by-bit, by the surrounding darkness.

On this class-skipping morning, I went to the restroom to brush my teeth, only to find a lifeless and fatigued face, which I hardly recognized, appearing in the mirror. This time, I heard the unuttered sigh and the roaring rebuke from the Holy Spirit: "Is this the college life you want? Do you think it's meaningful to continue this lifestyle?" Suddenly, God shot a Scripture into my mind like thunder: "The sorrows of those will increase who run after other gods." As if awakened from a long coma, I opened up my eyes, and saw the real self deep inside me: unconsciously, I had made an idol out of dancing, and had let it take over my life, in order to satisfy my selfish desire for man's praise and admiration. Facing God's glorious radiance, I had to let go of my idol. That morning, I decided to quit the Street Dance Club, and my tightening fists, that once tried to grab onto every part of my life, were warmed and loosened by God's light of life.

After leaving the Street Dance Club, I had more time to concentrate on my service in the CCC Fellowship, as well as on my schoolwork. During the rest of my college life, I began to see God's plan for me: "Therefore go and make disciples of the people you meet, teaching them to obey everything I have commanded you."

The people around me needed Christ. In the English Department, because of the liberal and tolerant atmosphere, the professors were proud of being atheists, humanists, and leaders of homosexual movements. In class, they talked about their suspicion of the sovereignty of God, and criticized traditional Biblical teaching. Consequently, students generally adopted the same characteristics, and became critical and suspicious toward rules, authority and tradition.

However, on the other hand, this liberal policy became a protection and an access for me to share my faith freely and directly. There was a course on Biblical literature, in which I used my term paper as an argument to show God's sovereignty, righteousness, justice, and mercy in the book of Genesis, to my teacher. In that paper, I discovered surprisingly that God was integrating my academic research with my faith, creating a brand new access to sharing the Gospel.

Within the following three and a half years, God continued to mold me and shape me into the vessel He would use for a greater task. During that time, I became the leader of the CCC Fellowship, cooperating with other Christian fellowships from different churches. We began to have prayer meetings among fellowship leaders and counselors, and organized various campus-wide evangelistic activities, all for the same purpose, to bring a spiritual revival to our campus.

Amazingly, however, in the midst of the busy ministry schedule, my schoolwork had not become an obstacle. On the contrary, it became a new avenue for me to share the Gospel, sharing the Gospel through my papers and academic research. Studying and researching were no longer dry and dull routines, but a chance for me to see the presence of God and the reality of people's spiritual hunger. When studying the history of European literature and humanistic philosophy, I saw how people had first denied the sovereignty of God, then Christ's salvation, and eventually stepped onto the path of atheism and agnosticism until the world was shattered by wars, as people continued their endless search for Truth among the ashes of broken civilization.

In the course Literature Criticism, those great philosophers and authors told us about the ultimate beauty and sublimity of truth, but did not know where to find it, just as was expressed in Pilate's question: "What is truth?" On seeing the pathetic spiritual condition of fallen humanity, I

was urged, in my paper, to let the whole world know that Jesus is the way, which impressed my professors.

In addition to witnessing in the academic field, I began to write Chinese Christian rap songs, hoping to share the Gospel with young people through this unique art form, pouring the Word of God straight into their hearts. Later, this simple idea became my first music album-- The Way to Eternity. Just before I graduated, God wondrously integrated my family background, my faith, my schoolwork, my hobby and my personality, making me His vessel to help fulfill the Great Commission in this ever-changing generation.

> *"Gaining what you can't keep to gain what you can't lose."*
> *—The Law of Rewards, by Randy Alcorn*

When I look back on all those years, I finally understand Christ's teaching in Mark 8:35: "For whoever wants to save his life will lose it, but whoever loses his life for me and for the Gospel will save it." As I faced my own mistake and others' misunderstanding, I gave up my friends' support and approval in order to do the right thing. When faced with the impulse of my selfish desire, I let go of the seemingly precious chance to have a romantic relationship, and at the height of expressing my talent, I abandoned the chance to become the dancing king on the stage. Yet, all those temporary losses were insignificant compared with the eternal treasure that I gained.

As I asked for my teacher's forgiveness, I learned to humble myself and love others with the love of Christ. In the process of guarding my heart, I saw the importance of self-restraint and the purity of friendship. Moreover, in giving up dancing five hours a day, I began to experience the life-long fruitfulness of serving God alone.

If I had determined to hold grudges against my teacher, then my heart would have been filled with bitterness and pride; if I had given flowers of passion, I would have fallen into the swamp of temptation along with the girl. If I had tried my best to grasp the dazzling thrill of dancing, then I wouldn't ever have seen God's wonderful plan, which was far brighter and much more colorful than the spotlight on the stage.

Now, after graduating from Central University, I continue to share my faith through my rap songs, which I have put on the multi-media blog called "Street Voice". At the same time, I cooperate with different churches in evangelistic concerts, and work with some teachers and volunteer moms to deliver messages about building character to high schools and elementary schools.

Looking back, what my parents did right was that when facing the drastic differences between the two generations, they cared more about the intentions and the spiritual meanings rather than appearance; they accepted those differences as long as they weren't against the truth nor arousing lust and temptations, which not only enabled me to develop my own style, i.e. baggie T shirts and jeans, but at the same time gave me a clear bottom line of God's truth.

Samuel Lee grew up in a Christian worker's family. He graduated from Central University of Taiwan, served as student worker, internet gospel writer, and is now currently in military service. He hopes to join his parents' organization, Campus Crusade for Christ, as a full time worker.

Tears to Joy

God's Grace

Beth Long Turner

I picked up my tray, walked over to my "Family Group" and was introduced. I looked across into a pair of blue eyes and thought "Danger, stay away from that one." I stuck my face down (like a good Taiwanese) and quickly ate my dinner. A few days later, this blue-eyed guy came up to me and asked me why I was here at this school...

This is my story...I was born in Hawaii to a military doctor and a mom who was only twenty-one. After two years and two more children who were born, we moved to Vietnam, where my dad began his career as a missionary doctor. This was against many people's advice, as it was in the middle of the Vietnam War. When I was 7 years old, Vietnam was taken over by the Communists, and we had to move. This is when we moved to Taiwan. Most of my years from that point on were spent there. I graduated from Morrison Academy, and for many years, considered Taiwan as my true home.

High school for me was a great time. I thought life would never change. There was no such thing as detention, that I can recall (of course there was no helmet rule, either!), and it wasn't cool to cheat, drink, smoke, swear, or lie, so we didn't do any of these things. The school was smaller, and many of my friends came from families similar to mine.

I look at my life and try to find a way to describe the different stages. I love music, it affects me strongly, and so I've decided to use it to categorize the different periods of my life. For an example of what life was like for us back then, I want to share some snapshots with you. Let's call high school the "Amy Grant" era...at least at home. My dad actually used to edit Amy Grant albums before he would let me listen to them. At school, it was Boston, Journey, and the Imperials. Great 80's stuff...

When choosing colleges, most of us didn't get to see the school we were going to. I was interested in sports and wanted to see how far I could go with playing volleyball, so I applied to a small Christian school in Rochester, New York. Because I was considered a state resident, I could get state aid. I was independent and self-confident, and my parents didn't know any better, so I talked them into letting me go back to the States without them that first year. Now, you have to realize this was before the Internet, before cell phones, and all that you use to communicate with. I mean, really, how many of you actually use your home phones to call someone? I arrived at school several months later, about 6 hours away from my grandparents. I met my roommate and settled into school.

To fly through those years, which were actually the greatest influence on the next 10 years of my life, I'll give just a few illustrations. After my first year, the school dropped their volleyball program. I played basketball (as bad as I was) and was one of 6 players on the team. It was a big lifestyle change. After being involved in sports every day for 2+ hours at Morrison, this became a huge disappointment to me. On the good side, it was the first time I'd ever eaten Nachos and cheese, Buffalo wings, mozzarella sticks or ice cream flavors other than chocolate, vanilla, strawberry, or taro. This stage I call the UB40 era....you know, "Don't Worry, Be Happy." As bad as things got, without someone who understood, I managed to cover it all with a smile.

There were other things that were new to me: I didn't know that senior guys routinely picked up freshmen girls, and as I spent all my time in the gym, my friends were mostly basketball players, many of whom had recently been recruited from inner-city New York and knew the name of Jesus as only a swear word. I had never learned to keep my own sleep and study hours (the dorm scheduled all of that for us through our senior year) and so I thought, "Why sleep? It's just a waste of time!" In years to come, this lack of sleep became a pattern and contributed to a lot of problems I encountered. There was no evening curfew and who doesn't like to be out in the middle of the night? My roommate taught me that if I threw up what I'd eaten, I wouldn't gain weight. I knew this was bad for my body (besides the fact that it didn't help me keep the weight off) so I quit after about 3 or 4 months, though it took me 2 years to completely stop throwing up.

I tried to communicate my struggles with my parents, but being the oldest child, I didn't want to seem too helpless or be an inconvenience to them, so after one appeal to them to "get me out of here, I want to come home," and one encouragement from them to "hang in there, it will get better" (like most parents would do), I didn't ask them again. I had to write a letter to them to communicate, because there was only a pay phone at the end of the hall. If they called, I would either be gone or no one would answer the phone, or if someone did, they wouldn't bother looking for me.

I tried to take a bus to my grandparents' the first vacation, and after trying for 45 minutes to get a taxi to pick me up out in the countryside where the school was located; I gave up and told my grandmother I was staying at school. Needless to say, there were many lonely moments during those years. I changed roommates after the first semester, and my second roommate was also bulimic and ended up leaving school because of it after that semester. My next roommate was a senior and wasn't around much. My next roommate was engaged to my friend and sleeping with his best friend. My last roommate was a great girl, with whom by that time

I had very little in common with. This era ended with my flash-in-the-pan interest in Queen Latifa and the Beastie Boys... I'm afraid to say. All this music covered up a lot of unhappiness. I worked 4 jobs my sophomore year and don't remember that year...honestly don't remember it...because I slept so little. I dated on and off, mostly guys who didn't stick around when they found out I planned on staying a virgin.

After I graduated, I stayed in Rochester to work, and at that point started sleeping with my boyfriend. I had to move after a year to care for my grandmother, and after she passed away, I came back home to Taiwan for a while. I met a guy I had dated earlier, a MK from another country, and when he expressed an interest in getting back together; I was honest with him as to where I was at, and what I had done. His reply was, "Well, I guess we'll never get together then."

After this, I figured it was too late; I had ruined my chances and there was no going back to a pure life, so upon returning to the States, I began a cycle of living that was easy to get into and hard to get out of. I worked as a traveling nurse, moving every 3-6 months to a new job. I would try to stay to myself, wanting to do the right thing, but being alone was a struggle for me, with my personality. I would usually end up hanging out with other girls like myself who traveled, and since we worked evenings, we would go out afterwards to the only places open at midnight...the bars. I call this my country music stage...you know, "There's a tear in my beer because I'm crying for you dear"....OK, I'll spare you that.

I ended up in Louisiana (that's another long story) and started dating yet another guy. I stayed there for about a year. His family had some problems and his father finally offered us 1000 USD to elope. I know it sounds ridiculous, but it's true. This is where I need to tell you that sometimes we have to hold on to some crazy things to make the right decisions, but we hold on to them anyway. I knew my mom would want to have a wedding for me, and this made me say, "No, probably not the best idea" (there were so many other better excuses, like "You don't have a job," and "you're only 20," or "you come from a family with a history of mental illness."). I went through a time of deep depression then. The guy was unhappy, and I kept trying to make him happy...girls, this will never work. If he's not happy without you, he won't be happy with you...Oh, sorry, guys...same thing goes for you...you cannot be someone's happiness!

The other weight upon me was my guilt. Once we know what is right, we can never be free when we are doing what is wrong. I was sitting at my table one night in tears and contemplating how I could end my life. Again, the excuse I found was strange, but again, whatever it takes to get us through these times is a gift. My parents were coming back to the States for Christmas and the whole family was going to be together in NY, so my excuse was, "I don't want to ruin their Christmas, and I'll wait till afterwards to kill myself." When I was with them, I was able to share with my sister what was going on, and then with my mom. My dad took me out to breakfast the next day and talked to me about the idea of surrounding myself with people who would encourage me and help me do the right thing. He encouraged me to apply to a grad school in South Carolina that was for anyone wanting to study the Bible or become a missionary. Right then, I was so miserable, I would have agreed to anything. Well, once I agreed, there was no going back. The problem was, I still had 7 months before I had to be there.

I returned to Louisiana, packed up my stuff, and moved to Florida. Now began my AC/DC stage. I love the music, but there is something about it that makes you want to break things. =) It was another time of little to no sleep. I would work 12 hour shifts at night and then sleep a few hours and play at the beach all day. I started drinking more and also smoking. In the midst of all this, I applied to the Bible college which stated that drinking, although not prohibited in the Bible, was not to be done excessively and smoking had negative effects on the body, which didn't please God. We can lie to ourselves, we can lie to others, but it will never change what is true! I didn't get into any other drugs, and I'm honestly not sure why. My nurse friends had lots of antidepressants and offered them to me, but it wasn't something I was as easily tempted by. My temptations were relationships, getting attention and security from relationships.

By the end of the summer, I got into the college, and only went because I had promised my dad many months before that I would go. I arrived the first day and set up my dorm room (and snuck my cat in there too, which was against the rules) and then plugged in my AC/DC and wondered, "What on earth am I doing here?" I was supposed to room with an older girl from Taiwan, but she hadn't arrived. I heard the door next door open and the girl in there started singing at the top of her lungs...praise songs. I thought to myself..."Thank goodness, I don't have to room with her!"

Not five seconds later, there was a knock at the door, and the RA (the student in charge of the floor) was at the door. "I'm sorry," she says, "But your roommate won't be here for a while, and we would like to have you move next door."

I couldn't believe it, so I looked around my room and said, "Well, I'm already moved in, can't she move in here?" I'm sure she was taken aback by my sullenness...most people in this place were so happy to be there!

"Uhhh, no, I'm sorry, you need to move into her room." So I picked up a few things and walked into the room next door.

Here was this girl, (pure as the driven snow) who looked about 18 and she throws her arms around me and says, "Beth, it's so nice to meet you!" lifts her hands and looks up and says "Thank you, Jesus!" and then hugs me again..."I've been praying for you ever since I found out I was coming here!"

I was puzzled to say the least, "But how did you know I was going to be your roommate?"

She said, "Oh, I didn't, I just prayed for whoever God was giving me!" and once again she raised her hands and looked at the ceiling and said, "Thank you, God!"

At that point, my conversation with God was, "ARE YOU CRAZY??? Why on earth did you put me here? We have nothing in common...You have no idea what you're doing!"

Well, Alice (in Wonderland, as I liked to call her) was what she seemed to be. She woke early, singing (fortunately she had a good voice) and I covered my head with my pillow to try to get some more sleep. I was miserable, she was happy as a lark.

I walked into the dining hall the first night and sat by myself. A girl walked up to me and asked me what my name was, looked on a list and said, "Oh, you're in that Family Group over there, you can join them!" (Family Group, what is this, some kind of cult?)

"Uh, no thanks, I'm just going to eat and leave."

Once again, that puzzled look of "Why is she so grouchy?" "No, I'm sorry, you need to join them, someone else will be using this table"...so I moved.

I picked up my tray, walked over to my "Family Group" and was introduced. I looked across into a pair of blue eyes and thought "Danger, stay away from that one," stuck my face down (like a good Taiwanese) and quickly ate my dinner. A few days later, this blue-eyed guy came up to me and asked me why I was here at this school...my answer seemed to puzzle him (because I definitely wasn't going to say...I've been living in sin, I've been so depressed I that I had wanted to kill myself, so I'm here against my better judgment to pass the time until I can leave) so I thought of the next best answer..."Ummm...I'm a nurse, and sometimes my friends have difficult questions about Christianity, so I want to be able to give them the right answers."

Again...the puzzled look. As I got to know this guy over the next couple of weeks, I decided he was ok, but still stayed away from any kind of personal discussions. After the first week of orientation, a feeling of dread slowly came over me. I had a horrible fear, and finally confessed to my roommate, who, although she was not like me, did like me – I knew this by her actions and words towards me – I confessed that it was possible I might be pregnant. This is where I began to see the hand of God upon my life...she said (with no shock or amazement because she had been a Crisis Pregnancy Counselor for 2 summers) "Well, there's one way to find out...I'll go with you to get a pregnancy test." She sent me to take the test and told me, "I'll be here praying for you..." As I came back into the room, she stood to her feet, tears streaming down her face, and said, "God told me that you're not to worry, He has everything under control!"

My response was, "No! He doesn't...I'm pregnant."

As I laid there that day, I gave up 2 things. The first thing I gave up was ever marrying a godly, good husband and the 2nd thing I gave up was ever going back to Taiwan to live and work.

There was a knock at the door and the girl across the hall came in, knelt next to me and asked me what was wrong. I poured out my heart to her, and then looked up to see that it wasn't the girl I thought, it was the RA in charge of the floor. I would have never told her I had plans to run away, as far as I could get. She said, "I know what to do" and she left and got the Resident Director, an older woman who knelt by me and said, "Remember Beth...all things work together for good to those who love God and are called according to His purposes."

"It's not possible;" I said, "there is nothing good about this."

Later that day, I ended up telling the guy I was friends with about what had happened...it took 2 hours of talking before I admitted what was going on, and I waited as I was sure he would say, "Then I guess there is nothing else I can do," but instead, he asked me, "Where are you now?" When I asked him to clarify, he asked "In relationship to God, where are you now?"

I spoke what I knew to be true, but did not feel..."God says that if we ask forgiveness from Him, we are forgiven and He removes our sins."

His response was, "Then how can I do anything different from what God has done for you?"

Another miracle I found during that time was the realization that when I had gone to a doctor who specializes in pregnancy and birth a month before, he had diagnosed my symptoms as adjusting to taking the pill, and had never thought to give me a pregnancy test. If I had taken it then, there was a high chance I would have had an abortion, like my former 2 roommates had done. Instead, a month later found me surrounded by people who loved me, cared about me and saw God working in my life.

7 months later, my daughter Grace was born...what better name could I have given her? God showed me Himself and His character repeatedly through those around me who accepted me where I was, and urged me to give myself wholly to God. I ended up marrying the blue-eyed guy when my little girl was 4 months old, and he adopted her as soon as he could. So you see, this story isn't really about me...it's really about God.

If it were just about me, I would tell you that my part included the sin and the consequences, for there were great consequences for my sin, even today, though you don't see them, they are there - when you think of the wasted years when you could have been following God, when you get the horrible feeling in the pit of your stomach as you realized you lied to someone without thinking, and have to go back, ask forgiveness, and keep moving toward being a truth-teller always, when you get a craving for something you developed a habit for in the past...and it returns out of the blue on a day when you haven't thought of it for 4 years, when memories pop into your mind that you wish with all your heart were not a part of you, when you lose the years of just being a couple because you already have children to care for, when your daughter's eyes well up with tears as, in 7th grade biology, she finally realizes the truth that she doesn't have her daddy's genes, but some stranger she will never know...her question is, "Then why am I so much like Dad?"

Oh, that the world can see our lives, see our God and ask the same question...you are sinful people, born sinful, living in a sinful world...then why are you so much like Him? Unlike any other religion, ours is the only one where a holy God sees His beloved children, knows that there is no way we can reach Him, and He finds a way to reach down to us, to span the great distance between us and Him. What can we do for Him...as praise and worship to Him for all He has done for us?

This is it: Don't be overwhelmed by trying to "live the Christian life." When you look back on your life and you want to know that you "fought the good fight," "ran the race well," "did what was right in the eyes of the Lord,"...you will see that it was a series of moment by moment decisions added up to a whole life. In this moment, I choose to do what will honor my God because I have very few ways of repaying Him for all that He has done for me. In this moment, I will say "no" to that sin, and because I know that my God smiles upon me. In this moment, I will choose joy instead of fear. Knowing that it pleases God, in this moment I will resist that craving, that temptation, that sin. I will choose to forgive; I will choose to ask for forgiveness; I will choose truth in this moment...and someday look back at all the moments together and realize that a holy life was the result of obedience moment by moment. When I think of God's love for me...this is what I see...a Father who loves us, no matter where we are, where we've come from, where we've been...a Father who delights in the very existence of His child.

———

Beth and her husband and three children reside in Taiwan. They have been serving as Dorm Parents at Morrison Academy, Taichung, Taiwan for over 10 years.

Do You Wish to Get Well?

Moses Sung

"I won't be well, don't expect me to ever be well again!" Moses screamed wildly to his mother. He was totally out of control.

Mrs. Sung's heart was broken. "Moses, please don't act like that. Promise me, you will never ever attempt to take your own life again," she pleaded with her son.

"Why should I promise you?" he replied.

"Please think of your grandpa and grandma. They love you, and they are over 80 years old. If anything happens to you, they will die of broken hearts!" she said.

"I can't even care about my own life, so how could I be bothered with theirs' !" he exclaimed.

Ignoring his mother's shock, Moses spit out these words, causing his mother's heart to turn cold, and sending it to the bottom of the valley.

"You think I want to act like this? I can't help myself!" Moses mumbled, his heart mixed with agitation and anger, despair and weariness.

He decided to fall into the pit of the world of computer games. During those two years, that was his most familiar world. However, it led him into a pit of bitterness, one that he could not come out of by himself.

A Carefree Youth

From his childhood, Moses barely gained passing marks in his school work. However, he was always fortunate enough to be promoted to the next grade, and then to high school, and then to university. Finally, he was able to enroll in his desired major for graduate school, Psychology. Life had been smooth and he was quite self-confident. He did not care much about what others thought of him. Moreover, even though he grew up in church, Jesus had never been his Lord, and Moses chose to have control of his own life and to be his own master.

Moses never had to worry about his livelihood. In fact, his way of life was to escape whenever there was pressure. He left his home in Taipei went to Kaohsiung to pursue graduate studies. He felt like a bird out of the cage, and was so happy that no one would bother him. When pressures in life came, he began to indulge himself in computer games as an escape. Eventually he totally lost control of himself.

He not only abandoned his academic work, he also accrued a large amount of credit card debt. He even ignored his girlfriend's kind concern for him. Finally, his girlfriend was so heartbroken that she left him. It was then that he came to realize how serious the matter was, but he could no longer get her back. Moses could not bear the blow of losing his girlfriend, and got more and more hooked on internet games. Day and night he went in and out of the internet cafe, hoping to forget the pain of losing his loved one.

Going down, down, down......

Moses regained his senses, at least temporarily. But his bitter life had just begun.

"What has happened to me? Why do I wake up every morning with a wet face?" he asked himself one morning.

Ever since his girlfriend left him, Moses cried himself to bed every night. He thought this kind of feeling would pass, but it actually grew worse as the days went by. He not only cried himself to sleep, but woke up crying.

Finally, Moses said to himself, "I can't go on like this; I need to go for a check up at the hospital." Sure enough, the psychiatrist diagnosed him with depression. "Oh, it is over for me. I am so young, but I have gotten into depression. My whole life is ruined." Now, knowing that he had depression, Moses became even more depressed and began to 'give up on himself' and look down on himself. He took medication, but his depression grew worse instead of getting better.

Father's Heart

At first, the family did not know how bad Moses' situation had grown. However, just as paper cannot wrap up fire, so his "out of order" kind of lifestyle was discovered by his parents, and they realized that their son was far from well. Elder Sung hurried to Kaohsiung, and immediately paid off his son's credit card debts. He apologized to all offended parties on behalf of his son. He obtained a leave of absence for Moses, and brought him back to Taipei.

"How shall I face my relatives? Friends?" thought Moses. "They saw me happily going away to Kaohsiung for my graduate studies. Now I am returning with a leave of absence from the university." Returning to Taipei, Moses went into a deep, deep, depression.

Moses' father tried to comfort his wife by saying that when he was young, he, too, went astray. "It's a transition period, let us give our son more time and pray for him. He will come out of this."

However, Moses' mother was saddened to see Moses sit in front of his computer, day and night. He would not stop no matter how much she urged him. At night, she was tortured by the unending sounds of the striking of the keyboard. It was like the sound of a curse. Worry, anxiety, and a feeling of helplessness gripped his mother's heart. "Oh I can't take this anymore. If it were not for God, I wouldn't want to live anymore," she cried.

"Oh, no! Another patient of depression!" Elder Sung exclaimed, referring to his wife. He knew this was getting serious. "This cannot go on! Our family will be ruined!"

One night, his father could not tolerate it anymore, and he blurted out to his son:

"Do you know, your playing computer games day and night has broken your mother's heart? If you really want to play, ok, you can play your entire life!"

"I don't want to," said Moses. He really meant it. Yet, he had no control of himself. Moses read a report from the Medical Society of America saying that cases of depression would return 90% of the time, even though initially healed. "If I have to spend the rest of my life like this, I would rather die," he thought.

Moses suddenly thought of his father who asked him once, "Do you really believe in God?"

Moses' answer had always been, "Yes, I believe in God, of course. I am a pastor's son, after all. But, to put my life in God's hand's? No way." He wanted to be his own boss.

When he was still in Kaohsiung, he stood at the top of his school building more than once, wanting to jump off. One time in Taipei, he stood in the middle of a road, and caused a bus to screech to a halt. Moses stood there unmoved. Two people from the church saw him and brought him home. He felt he had no way out.

Suddenly, he thought of taking drugs. One night, he locked the door of his room, and swallowed a handful of pills. His hands began to shake, then his feet, then his face, and then his whole body shook. He was very conscious the whole night, but was determined he would not ask for help. He ended up shaking from midnight until dawn. Gradually, the effects of the drug wore off. He did not die, but collapsed.

The End of Man's Road, and the Beginning of God's

Because of this "suicidal" tendency in Moses, the doctor decided to put him into the psychiatric ward. With his parent's permission, he voluntarily checked into the hospital, thinking that this was his last chance. However, he was totally shocked at what he saw. "Why isn't this like other hospitals? Why is this so horrible? Patients have to take heavy doses of medication until they are numb."

When Moses discovered that this was not the same as other hospital wards, he was totally unprepared for it, and became utterly frightened. The next day, Moses climbed barefoot over the wall and ran off. The police got him and sent him back to the hospital. He was tied up and put into confinement. He was distressed and called home, saying he wanted to leave the hospital as quickly as possible.

"Oh God, my son has broken my heart into pieces. I am helpless, what should I do?" cried his mother. While she was praying, she heard God say to her, "You think you are in pain? Your son is in even more pain."

After this, Moses' mother adopted a new attitude towards this painfully long journey. She was determined to help her son, walk with him, and not focus on her own pain. The entire church was praying, earnestly and tearfully. The Sung family felt the love of dear brothers and sisters as their greatest source of support and care. The Sungs became aware that even they themselves, as pastors, can also feel helpless and weak. They grew to know God more - His eternal love, hope, and strength.

When father returned to Taipei from a ministry trip, he went to the hospital and found his son counseling other patients. He had been applying his knowledge of Psychiatrics, and the patients felt he understood them, and they liked him. Yet, Moses still could not help himself.

"In treating patients of depression, we can only treat 20% of them, using drugs to stop them from being suicidal. That's all," the psychiatric department head told them frankly. "The other 80% is up to the patient's personality. We have no other way. You have your faith, you can pray to your Jesus."

From this non-Christian doctor's mouth, the Sungs were amazed and rejoiced. With his father's help Moses checked out of the hospital and went home.

New Life

Though he had not been to church for quite a while, Moses knew that on the Wednesday night while he was in the hospital, the entire church had been praying earnestly for him. They continued to care for him. A counseling professor at the seminary began seeing him regularly. He felt loved and was touched. A brother in Christ asked him to come to church a few mornings a week to read the Bible together with him.

"Well, I will go, since I have nothing else to do." Four months went by, and Moses went from crying daily, to crying every two or three days a week, to once every one or two weeks. Moses was doing so much better, but not totally healed.

On December 19, 2003, on a cold winter night, Moses began crying all night. Afraid of disturbing his parents, he went outside and began walking along the dark alleys, softly singing hymns, hoping the hymns could strengthen him. Tears kept streaming down his face. He walked until dawn. This happened to be the day he would read the Bible with his mentor, so he went straight to church. He sat down and they began to read John Chapter 5, about a paralytic who had been sick for 38 years. "When Jesus saw him lying there, and knew he had already been a long time in that condition,"

Moses cried in his heart, "Jesus, do you see me? Do you know how much pain I have been in during these past two years?"

Jesus asked him, "Do you wish to get well?"

The Word went right into Moses' heart and he was so moved. He trembled with excitement and immediately responded in his heart, "Lord Jesus, I want to be healed, I want to be healed!"

"Get up, pick up your pallet and walk."

Now, tears came down Moses face, but this time they were tears of joy.

His mentor looked at him gently, with eyes beaming, and said, "Moses, do you know what? You are totally healed."

"Yes, yes, I know that I am healed!" Moses felt assured. Though he was still jobless and could not easily concentrate, he knew that he was healed. His heart had been changed and God had healed him!

Blessings in Disguise

From that day on, Moses did not take any medication anymore. Neither did he fall into depression again. He found his destiny. He applied to enter the same study program in another university in Taipei. This university was near his home. Moses was determined to equip himself to be a psychiatric doctor in order to help patients of depression.

Now, life is still full of pressures and hardships, but Moses believes that just as God helped him out of depression, God is able to carry him through every hardship.

Looking back, Elder and Mrs. Sung's hearts are full of thanksgiving, "Christians are not exempt from the trials of life, but God will grant us sufficient grace. Through this trial, we have learned more of God's love, and we are drawn closer to the hearts of suffering parents."

"Never give up hoping. The journey is painful, but God's grace is sufficient. With Him, we can walk together. We will come out of the past, and see healing happen." This is what the Sung family believes.

Moses Sung grew up in Taipei, Taiwan as a PK.

This story was first published (in Chinese) by Cosmic Light magazine of Taiwan. It was an interview with Moses. Translated by permission.

Spiritual Heritage
of TCKs

Spiritual Heritage of TCKs

Cindy Loong

Through my journey of reconciliation with God and my parents, I saw the glory of God shine through this deep well of my missionary heritage. Yes, this is who I am and where I belong! I believe that God is extending this invitation to all TCKs ... God's scales are heavy with the pain and sacrifice by pastors and missionary kids, whether or not they have made it completely through their pain yet. I believe TCKs are born to be world changers. So, let "Phase II" of Modern Missions begin!

Part One: Cultural Transitions

I had already shifted between the Eastern and Western cultures five times by the time I was fourteen years old. It may seem like an exciting life to some, but for me, these were critical points in my development that left me feeling like a confused iceberg (see "The Iceberg"). I moved so frequently during my developmental years, I struggled with cultural balance. The importance of cultural balance is stated well by Kohl in David Pollock's book,

> "Once we have stayed in a culture long enough to internalize its behaviors and the assumptions behind them, we have an almost intuitive sense of what is right, humorous, appropriate, or offensive in any particular situation. Instead of spending excessive time worrying if we are dressed appropriately for a business appointment, we can concentrate on coming up with a new business plan. Being "in the know" gives us a sense of stability, deep security, and a sense of belonging ... we may not understand why cultural rules work as they do, but we know how our cultures work.

Conversely, during transition, we have to learn and relearn the basic rules by which the world around us is operating. Our energies are spent in surviving rather than thriving. It's as if we are still figuring out the fingering for the scales on the piano while others around us are playing a Rachmaninoff concerto. Being out of cultural balance leaves us struggling to understand what is happening rather than fully participating in the event." (p.42)

My developmental years were full of difficulties because of the lack of cultural balance. No matter how hard I tried, I could never keep up with the surrounding culture. Just as Kohl and Pollock describe it, I experienced the full force of "iceberg confusion". Iceberg confusion can also be described using the analogy of acting in a play: Imagine being in scene 1 which is a living room. All of a sudden the set is changed and you find yourself in a forest instead. You can't watch TV anymore; you have to struggle for survival! The rules for your existence are suddenly changed. It throws you completely off balance. This is what it is like for TCKs, especially those who have experienced frequent moves.

Schools and Languages

My cultural struggles were in two main areas, in academics and language. I have a natural ability for studying the sciences. However, because of the influence of culture, I have not been able to attain to the level that I would have if I had stayed in one place. I have often regretted this, but God has shown me that in the end, He has more than compensated for my lack of achievement in the sciences. Another area affected by cultural struggles was language. I am currently trilingual in English, Mandarin, and Cantonese. People often admire my language capabilities, but many do not know the pains that I went through to overcome my language struggles.

Transition One: Changing Sets from East to West

My first language was Chinese. However, at age four, my native tongue was to change dramatically. My parents had to go to Colorado for missionary training for three months that summer. I remember trying my best not to let my mom go to the airport. (Prior to the 90's, Western mission agencies were very strict about candidates in training coming without their children. Thankfully, they have dropped that policy since the 90's). When I knew my crying was not working, I gave in to my English speaking cousins, who took me to their home in New York. My cousins tried their best to take care of me. None of this, however, could resolve my underlying feelings of complete loss and disorientation.

Unbeknownst to me, God was allowing a change of settings for the next three months: East to West, Chinese to English. The only thing familiar from the first setting was my sister, Mabel. However, even this was suddenly changed! Mabel had attended nursery in the States, and by then she was somewhat fluent in English. When my sister started speaking English to my relatives, I was even more bewildered. Now I was truly alone. I lost much weight because of the stress of cultural adjustment. It broke my mother's heart when she saw me at the end of that summer.

By then, I had picked up English as my native tongue, but it was not without its costs. In years to come, Mabel and I would experience a communication gap with my parents because of this. David Pollock talks about this phenomenon in *The TCK Experience*. (p. 118) I particularly remember my father's great efforts to speak English to us. We, in turn, tried many times to switch back to Cantonese without success.

Transition Two: Changing Sets from West to East

When I was six years old, my parents were called to the mission field of Taiwan. For weeks they would prepare my sister and I for this transition by telling us about the food and fun places, but they didn't tell us about the difficulties of cross-cultural adjustment, nor helped us grieve about leaving the United States. There were no resources regarding cross-cultural transition available for missionaries back then. Moreover, they were typical Chinese and were not as free to express deep feelings and emotions.

The time came for us to board the plane and before I knew it, we landed in Taipei. When I woke up at 2am in the morning, my body knew that something was up! It felt like morning in my body, but the setting was nighttime. Once again, I was pulled away from one set and placed into a Mandarin speaking drama.

In a few weeks' time, the drama would intensify, as I would be placed in a Mandarin first grade classroom. To my surprise, my parents began speaking in Mandarin to the people around them! Culturally, I felt they had changed, too. They changed from being more Americanized to becoming more Chinese. Even their style of disciplining my sister and I also changed to a more Chinese style. My dad had often been very Chinese in the way he disciplined my sister and I. However, in Taiwan he became even more Chinese. One time, he scolded me in public in Mandarin. I was so shocked because I had not seen this part of him before, both in language and in culture. When I found out we would be returning to the States soon, I looked at the calendar everyday expectantly. When my mother noticed this, she scolded me for doing it. In her own way, she was trying to keep me focused on life in Taiwan, but she did not know that the calendar was my only connection to my cultural home.

My sister was placed in an English speaking missionary kids' elementary school; we had less and less in common, even though we were still speaking English to each other. It was disturbing to me, but probably also strange for her to see me walking in every afternoon with a Chinese uniform, and loads and loads of homework that she never had to do. In many aspects, we had different "sets" during that year in Taiwan. I was alone in my set.

That year, I felt like I had no emotional support for what I was going through. My parents tried to help me adjust in many practical ways. However, I still felt very lonely. Later on, I was to find out that the losses experienced by TCKs could be compared to the death of a loved one. Upon flying to Taiwan, I had lost a whole world, but since I didn't have emotional support, I buried these emotions. In years to come, my Taitung experience would affect the way I viewed Asia and the Chinese culture. By the time I was in university, I had firmly decided that I would never go back to a Chinese speaking culture.

I had a profound spiritual life the year before I went to Taitung. I learned to pray to God and felt close to Him. However because everything in my set changed upon arriving Taiwan, and I had very little emotional support, I felt like even God Himself did not care anymore. I felt like He didn't hear my prayers. Later on, I found out God had been faithful to me, but it was my feelings toward my parents, my sister and my environment that caused me to lose my trust in God. Because of my feelings, here are the lies I believed, "When I experience grief, loss and culture shock, God is not with me and He does not help me. He doesn't care how I feel and He won't be there to see me through. Moreover, significant people in my life will not be there for me as well. I have to do it on my own." Because of these lies, I adopted insecurities in dealing with the many cross-cultural adjustments that were to come even after this one.

I was not doing well under the stress of academics, even at first grade. I was constantly anxious because I didn't know the rules of this set called "strict disciplinary and exam-oriented Taiwan education system." I didn't know how to express my fears. After summer vacation, I would describe the vacation as being "wasted," meaning "regretful," because I dreaded going back to school.

Transition Three: Moving to Singapore

Now, Singapore is an interesting place because many cultures are represented there, and most people speak English, so I thought language would not be an issue. However, besides language, there were the hidden beliefs, values, assumptions, and thought processes that I just did not get. In Kohl's language, our icebergs were not getting along, they were clashing under the water level!

To deal with this stress, I buried myself in books. Once again, I was anxious because I didn't know the rules of this set called "exam-oriented Singapore education system." I genuinely believed threats from teachers that if I failed the elementary school exit exams, I would be doomed for my secondary career. I didn't know how to express my fears. I had experienced too many school systems and changes to trust any of them. I remember in some instances having to ask my teacher two or three times about a certain thing before I was completely convinced of was what was expected of me!

I tried hard to fit in. I hid my differences. I decided I would quit being different and blend in completely. I looked like a local (even had the typical school girl hair cut), and even in behavior and study habits I succeeded in becoming almost completely Singaporean. However, underlying cultural differences between the environment and my own "cultural iceberg" could not be resolved. I was not even close to being local on the inside! I didn't get their jokes. I didn't understand their rules for relationships. I experienced a gap in communication and that was more difficult to hide.

My parents, who were busy with missionary training in a community setting, and adjusting to a new ministry and cultural setting themselves, were not always available for me. One time I wrote in my journal, "I don't have anyone to talk to about my problems at school. So here they are. Mom used to be a good one but now she seems to be so busy and I can't really find a right time to tell her."

My parents tried to speak Chinese with us. I wrote in my journal, "We went to the Hawker Center and after that I began to worry. My father said to Mabel that she had to speak to him in Chinese. He spoke to me in Mandarin too. I cried." I had experienced too many crossing of cultures and switching of languages; the thought of changing again was just too overwhelming. In fact, cultural changes affected me so deeply that around this time I began to develop TMJ (temporo-mandibular joint) disorder.

Transition Four: East to West

Mabel went to boarding school one year before I did. When I came the next year, she would comfort me with stories about her own adjustment which she went through her first year. She would say, "Don't worry, Cindy. When I first came, they didn't know what I was talking about either." We suffered because our English was not the same kind of English as the rest of the kids in boarding school.

Wounded and Healed

By my early twenties, the situation with my TMJ disorder had become medically impossible to cure, with surgery as the only option for me, yet without any guarantee for recovery. However, God was ready to orchestrate a "double-combo" crisis intervention in my life.

At this time, many of my parents' supporting churches and many of their close friends were praying for me. Meanwhile, my sister took me to Mott Auditorium in Pasadena where there was a revival meeting. One evening, the guest speaker delivered a dynamic message. Toward the end, he said, "I have a feeling that God wants to do a great work of healing tonight." He then proceeded to call out several medical cases that needed attention. The first case he described was, "There is a lady in the audience who has soreness in the left side of her mouth, in the gums, and she has had problems eating for quite a while." He went on to describe more details of my situation!

In complete awe, I stepped out to the front to receive prayer. During the prayer, I could sense my lower jaw being moved around several times. At the end of the prayer, I moved my jaw as my dentist usually asks me to do at his clinic. There was no grating, which had been one of the symptoms of the TMJ disorder. Because of God's perfect timing, my mother was there to witness this miracle first hand. News of my healing soon reached friends and churches that prayed for me. To God be the glory. I was so grateful to Him for healing me!

The very next week, I visited my dentist, Dr Ott. After examining my jaw with the usual tests, he concluded that the "membrane had indeed slipped back over the condyle, in between the bones," which I had been praying for all this time. In fact, my lower jaw had shifted so much that my lower front teeth no longer contacted the splint above. Dr Ott was truly amazed and admitted that this was the first miracle case he had ever witnessed in his clinic. I praised God for what He had done in my life, and surprising me with the power of His Spirit. However, I was soon to discover that this was only the beginning of my healing journey.

Part Two: Discovering my Spiritual Heritage

Around the time of the healing of my TMJ disorder, I began to learn about prayer, spiritual heritage, and revival, from my pastor Lou Engle of Harvest Rock Church. In his book *Digging the Wells of Revival*, he shares,

"God has been putting such a hunger in me to ignite people's passion to discover their spiritual genealogy and heritage and to receive a spiritual inheritance and identity from those great forefathers and mothers who went before us." (p. 30)

He quotes John Dawson's description about Britain:

"The vacant-eyed punkers and young urban professionals of British cities are the great-grandchildren of Livingston, Wesley, Whitefield, Booth, Wycliffe, Fox, Studd, and Taylor. The lives of these great heroes of the faith were intercessory acts. Their prayers still ascend before the throne of God. When God weighs Britain in the balance, the scales are heavy with missionary martyrs who gave their lives in Africa and China" (p. 32).

The writer teaches that when people begin to claim their spiritual inheritance of a past revival or movement, God will send a movement of the Spirit again. This is what it meant by digging wells. My journey in searching the deeper meaning of my life and my spiritual heritage had only begun. It took me another decade before I fully synthesized my spiritual heritage, the meaning of my MK life and revival.

Crashing in Academics

After university, I went on to attempt medical school for half a year, only to fail all my exams at the end of the semester. It was a shock, but now looking back, I should have seen it coming. My system of survival in different educational settings finally crashed. At any rate, I just knew I could not do this school thing anymore. Upon news of this crisis, my parents suggested that I come back to Hong Kong to teach English, where they were ministering. However, for me, it was like going from bad to worse. Failing out of medical school was one thing. Having to go back to Asia was another thing. I could not believe that God would actually allow me to move to yet another Asian city, and be forced to speak another Asian language. What I resolved would never happen to me was happening right before my very eyes! Like Daniel in the Bible, who was suddenly exiled to Babylon, I felt very much imprisoned in my cultural circumstances. I felt could not rise to my Daniel calling.

I secured a job teaching English. However, it was a dreadful experience. There seemed no purpose to waking up every morning and going to teach English to a bunch of Cantonese speaking youths who could care less about English. The staff room was noisy and people were talking so fast that I could hardly think. Now I realize that God allowed all these massive cultural immersions so that I could be confronted with and eventually be healed from my past. The memories of each transtion, between the East to West, promptly and painfully surfaced each day I walked the streets of Hong Kong.

It may seem strange that at times I needed to consult my mom as how to dress for school. I would exclaimed in dismay, "I wore the wrong thing today! Everyone has switched to summer clothes and I am still wearing a turtleneck. " In California, a comfortable outfit could be worn all year round as long as one had a decent warm coat. No such convenience in Hong Kong. Every season brought a new wardrobe, thus the term "changing closet" every time the season changed from summer to winter and vice versa.

Talbot and Israel

A year later, I enrolled in Talbot Seminary and thoroughly enjoyed my studies and times of prayer with students, both local and Asians. After graduation, I spent two months in Israel. While listening to Hebrew University students shared about their family history of transitions and homelessness, it seemed to me that they were in fact TCKs with their spiritual roots all the way back to Abraham's time. They are truly sojourners!

Hong Kong Again

After Israel, I was quite prepared to settle in Los Angeles, yet felt like God was saying to me, "Stay in Hong Kong, your destiny lies in your determination to go through life here until I tell you it is time to move on." I found the reserve to stay in Hong Kong.

Since I had already begun speaking Cantonese, I thought this would be an easier transition. It turned out to be just as hard, because I was adding on other cultural elements and stressors. For the second time I got a job teaching English. This time, the kids were worse than in the first school! What was worse, I felt led by the Lord to to switch completely from English to Cantonese at home, and not just speaking a few phrases here and there. I had Cantonese "din" in the staff room, Cantonese at home, (even Cantonese TV), and Cantonese at church!   It proved to be a very difficult transition.

Friendship and Discipleship – Keys to a Good Transition

Along with cultural adjustment, I was also dealing with a new level of healing, which was hidden in my cultural struggles. I left my good friends and spiritual mentors in L.A. The unfamiliar Cantonese speaking church was bringing out anxieties that had been buried deep down inside. My pastor's wife asked me why was I always anxious and uneasy around her. I tried to deny this but I knew she was right, and I knew this was because everyone in that church knew who my parents were. I fervently hoped that I could make the breakthrough and get past being known as so and so's daughter. I wished to be known as who I really was. God surprised me near the end of my first year at the Shepherd International Church.

My best friend from childhood, Elaine, a Caucasian missionary kid, visited me during Christmas. Elaine and I went to the same MK school in Taitung. Back then, our moms were prayer partners and our dads did surgeries together. I felt no one except Elaine understood how I felt about living in

Hong Kong. However, even she could not help to bring me out of a situation that God had allowed and ordained.

Meanwhile, my friend Angela in Hong Kong, whom I gradually got to know, would say in Cantonese, "Your spirit is not coming out." I thought she described it very well. Even though I was part of the intercessors group, when time came for intercession, I found it hard to pray. How would they feel, so I thought, if they had to pray in English? It boggled my mind that they did not understand my difficulty. My pastor's wife told me that I should use English to pray and I found that impossible, since everyone else was praying in Cantonese.

Near the end of that year, I experienced the beginnings of breakthrough. The revival anointing in the city helped to give me spiritual fuel to plow through my process of healing and transformation. Everyone who wanted more of God, and wanted to see revival, was seeking spiritual renewal, MK or non-MK. I was blessed with a weekly ladies' discipleship group led by our pastor's wife. Every week we dealt with our "stuff". It was in this setting that I eventually found safety in sharing about my struggles and even receiving input from these ladies. I truly appreciated my good friends and this small group, which supported me along my journey of cultural transition and inner healing.

Healing Relationships with Parents

I entered into a season of healing and restoration. I started dismantling lies that I had believed in since childhood, which could be summarized as, "God has abandoned me." I replaced that lie with scripture and new experiences with God, feeling His love for the first time since I had arrived the mission field at age six. I realized that what the Bible says about God's faithfulness and compassion are really true. For the first time I was able to talk to my parents about past hurts and wounds. We cried together and talked through all those experiences. My dad prayed for me, and I prayed for him. I learned how to break generational patterns of relating to my parents.

My friends never judged me for my lack of fluency in Cantonese. This gave me courage to continue speaking. My dad opened up more to me because I was now speaking in his native tongue. He noticed every little bit of improvement and appreciated my efforts. Every new Cantonese phrase that I picked up was a new bridge between my parents and myself. I began to enjoy a friendship with my father that I never had before. I suddenly felt alive, like I was emerging into a new life in Hong Kong. I felt like how a child feels when he says something that communicates exactly what he/she means! I felt like I understood my parents in ways I had never conceived possible, because I was now thinking in their language. I began to understanding parts of my parents' Chinese culture that I had formerly been terrified of. I was also able to express my feelings and stand up for myself. Things I thought would be difficult to reconcile, would be reconciled in a few minutes' time, as soon as I found the right Cantonese phrase and tone of voice to say it. The walls of cultural and generational division began coming down. What I had once considered the worst fate – having to return to Asia, was becoming the greatest blessing of my life. I have to say that my parents were my greatest cheerleaders during this whole time!

Grandmother and Her Spiritual Heritage

I spent half a year staying with my grandmother, and in this way I learned even more Cantonese. My grandmother was gracious in talking with me, and explaining things I did not understand in the language. She also talked about the past. By Christmas time, I was speaking Cantonese better than ever. Moreover, I had received more of my grandmother's spiritual heritage as she talked about the days when she served the Lord in her church in China.

Not only did my Cantonese improve rapidly, so did my relationship with my grandmother. She often considers me the grandchild who understands her history the most.

Should I Pray and Preach in English?

One Saturday afternoon in the fall of 2004, I spoke at the youth service at my church. I talked about how to have a closer walk with God, but the youths were not getting it. It was basically a failure, and was devastating to me because it was the first time I had attempted preaching in Cantonese. I really did not want to ever try again. My friend, Angela, pulled me aside and said, "Cindy, when you went up there to speak, you became like another person. I don't think that is really you." I knew she was right. It was one of those awful moments when I knew that my cultural faking was not working.

That same evening, I went to a youth meeting. A young Chinese American pastor preached in English with a Cantonese interpreter. Soon the meeting turned into a prayer rally for revival on campuses. He preached: "Do you know that Christians founded most campuses in Hong Kong for the purpose of advancing the gospel? Its time to "dig the wells" of the Christian schools in Hong Kong and pray that God sends a revival!" When he said "dig the wells", something lit up in my spirit and I began to cry out to God, along with the entire yelling crowd, that God would dig the wells of these campuses. I felt like I had been beamed back in time to the Los Angeles prayer meetings, when I had prayed with my pastor Lou Engle!

After the meetings, I told my friend excitingly, "Did you hear me praying in English? That's how I used to pray!"

Immediately she responded, "Well, if that's the case, you should preach in English and I should translate for you." That day, I began using English again in prayer meetings. I preached in English in the youth service, while she translated.

Another youth worker exclaimed, "We are finally hearing from the other half of you!" Indeed, for two years, as I had been trying so hard to transition into Cantonese, the American part of me had been missing and left behind somewhere in the Pacific Ocean between Los Angeles and Hong Kong! However, after this incident, I dramatically improved in my ability to move freely between Cantonese and English in our prayer meetings. My prayers became more and more fluent and I could adjust my language based on the needs of the situation. My anointing in the prayer room went up dramatically. If I felt the need to pray in Cantonese, I would. Or if I felt led to communicate in English, I would pray in English. I was finally experiencing the fruit of three years of being in Hong Kong, and now I could effectively speak and pray bilingually!

Part Three : MK Identity and Phase II of Modern Missions

I moved back to the States for two years during 2005-2007. Being away from the Hong Kong culture helped me to have the space to realize that there were still issues that bothered me about the Cantonese culture, just like being in the States reminded me that there were things in the American culture that I was not comfortable with. As great as my transition into Hong Kong life and culture has been, I knew that the only way I had been able to transition was because of the powerful work of the Holy Spirit in my life, and in the city in which I was living. I accepted the fact that as an TCK I would not fully belong to one city, but could choose to settle where God called me. In the midst of cultural stress, Christ would be always there to comfort me with His presence, and to be a bridge between myself and the surrounding culture. And, once I experienced Christ as my bridge, I would ultimately be equipped to be a bridge between cultures!

MK Identity Through Reconciliation

Would the whole TCK problem have been solved if my parents speak both English and Chinese to us throughout our developmental years? Parents of TCKs may wonder about adopting this simple solution. "Let's just make sure they keep their Chinese," they might think. However, it would be ignorant to think of the issue as simple as this.

When a family embarks on a missionary career, they have chosen to be more stretched culturally, personally, and spiritually. This is not because God considers them better than others, but because God has chosen to reveal His grace through their lives. The pain of the relational, cultural and even spiritual gaps of the missionary life is part and parcel of the missionary calling. It is what missionary families sign up for.

The world that God came to save is a world of conflicts between cultures and people, that ranges from household tensions and societal disturbances, all the way up to wars and rumors of wars between nations and peoples. The first and foremost calling of the missionary family is to bring about reconciliation. God often stretches us in order to contain some of these conflicts. The challenge of every missionary family is to allow God to break us, and then to bring about reconciliation within our own lives and within the family, so that we might become ministers of reconciliation. (II Cor. 5:18)

I grew up with many missionary families around me. I came to realize there are few better places to know one's own inadequacies and God's grace than in the missionary calling. I have seen many parents and children, in their inadequacy, learn to lean on God's grace. A famous minister once said, "Everyone wants my calling and anointing, but no one wants my brokenness and pain." I have come to realize that it is this brokenness that qualifies one for ministry!

Similarly, I spent my post-college years seeking God about my identity and destiny. During the time my peers were developing their careers and families, it appeared as though I was not accomplishing much compared to them. However, I was in fact doing something very eternally significant – I was digging my revival well! God showed me that He purposed my life to be a display of His amazing grace. He allowed me to struggle intensely so that I could tell of His wondrous grace more profoundly. Having understood God's perspective, it has all been worthwhile. Likewise, my encouragement to struggling TCKs is to take heart and never give up on the process. God is there to see that you get through to the other side of your pain, even if you are about to give up. He will help you dig your revival well, and give you a revival that you have never imagined possible!

For the past ten years, I have made 2 Cor 4: 6-7 one of my mottos. "God shone light in our hearts to give the light of the knowledge of the glory of God in the face of Christ. But we have this treasure in earthen vessels, so that the surpassing greatness of the power will be of God and not from ourselves." Through my journey of reconciliation with God and my parents, I saw the glory of God shine through this deep well of missionary heritage. Yes, this is who I am and where I belong! I believe that God is extending this invitation to all TCKs.

Missionary Heritage and Phase II

On the evening of the first global day of prayer in Hong Kong in 2005, near the end, my father was asked to pray for world missions. I felt the effectiveness of his prayer, and I immediately knew the reason. Not only was he fluent in Mandarin (note: in Hong Kong few would pray publicly in Mandarin), he had also spent enough time in the Mandarin culture so that his Mandarin prayer carried authority! It was amazing! God began to speak to me about cultural heritage of MKs (my father is an MK, too!) When I heard him pray in this language, something lit up in me: MKs and TCKs need to start praying together all over the world, in their own languages, even without translation! I believe that TCKs are a key to revival. Together we represent the nations. When TCKs bring their cultural heritage and languages into the prayer room, this is in fact a realization of the many "tongues and tribes and peoples" that God will eventually gather around His throne (Revelation 7)! This is the moving of the Spirit at the end of the age!

I sense that God is ready to launch "Phase II" of modern missions. God is about to redeem the past of TCKs, to do double of what their parents could ever do. To get to Phase II, TCKs need to dig wells – to discover our unique spiritual roots and heritage.

Consider again, Lou Engle's book *Digging the Wells of Revival*, as he shares the following,

> "God has been putting such a hunger in me to ignite people's passion to discover their spiritual genealogy and heritage and to receive a spiritual inheritance and identity from those great forefathers and mothers who went before us" (p. 30).

I am convinced that the only way to get this inheritance is to walk right through the pain and face it head-on. I know I have had a hard dose of the hardships of a TCK's life, but many TCKs have had an even harder time than I, and are still reconciling with elements from their past. My guess is that the greatness of their heritage is proportional to their difficulties. My heart is to encourage them to press on. There is light at the end of the tunnel! Most people may not understand your path, but God knows and cares. He really has the best in store for you! You are not alone.

Consider John Dawson's quote once again:

"The vacant-eyed punkers and young urban professionals of British cities are the great-grandchildren of Livingston, Wesley, Whitefield, Booth, Wycliffe, Fox, Studd, and Taylor. The lives of these great heroes of the faith were intercessory acts. Their prayers still ascend before the throne of God. When God weighs Britain in the balance, the scales are heavy with missionary martyrs who gave their lives in Africa and China" (p. 32, Digging the wells of Reviral).

Surely God's scales are also heavy with the pain and sacrifice by TCKs, whether or not they have made it completely through their pain yet. I believe TCKs are born to be world changers. So, let "Phase II" of Modern Missions begin!

_____